SWIDDEN CULTIVATION AND THE DEVELOPMENT PROGRAMMES IN NORTH-EAST INDIA

SWIDDEN CULTIVATION AND THE DEVELOPMENT PROGRAMMES IN NORTH-EAST INDIA

(A Study Among the Karbis of Assam)

G.N. DAS

AKANSHA PUBLISHING HOUSE
NEW DELHI-110 059 (INDIA)

AKANSHA PUBLISHING HOUSE
R 37-B, Vani Vihar, Uttam Nagar
New Delhi - 110 059

Swidden Cultivation and The Development Programmes in North-East India

First Edition 2001

ISBN 81-87606-08-8

[The responsibility for facts stated, opinion expressed or conclusions reached, is entirely that of the Author. The publisher bears no responsibility for them.]

PRINTED IN INDIA

Published by M.P. Misra for Akansha Publishing House, New Delhi and Printed at Mehra Offset Press, Delhi.

In Memory of My

Mother, Golap Prabha Das

and

Brother, Pradip

CONTENTS

FOREWORD

I am happy to learn that Dr.Girindra Nath Das has arranged for the publication of the book titled, *Swidden Cultivation and the Development Programmes in North-east India (A study among the Karbis of Assam).*

The book is substantially based on his doctoral dissertation. It is a commendable addition to our knowledge of Economic anthropology with special reference to some socio-economically relevant aspects of the age-old practice of shifting axe cultivation vis-a-vis the Government-sponsored *Integrated Jhumia Development Programme* (IJDP).

Nowhere else we find the close inter-relationship between ecology, economy, technology of production and society better visible than among the swiddening population.

Swidden cultivation, also known as 'Slash and burn' or shifting cultivation represents a distinct stage in the history of man's exploitation of his environment. It seems to have been well established during the neolithic period more than 10,000 years ago. It has been reinforced as a system continually with experience of the people practising it. It has been enriched by the exuberant spirit of the people living in close proximity with nature. According to Food and Agricultural Organization, it is defined as, "the custom of cultivating clearance scattered in the reservoir of natural vegetable (forest or grass or wood land) and of abandoning them as soon as the soil is exhausted and this includes in certain areas the customs of shifting homesteads in order to follow the cultivators, searching for new lands". It is estimated that all over the world around 200 million people derive their food crops by practising shifting cultivation over some 3600 million hectares of land.

Swiddening is widely practised in the hill areas of North-east, Southern Orissa and Northern Andhra Pradesh. It is also prevalent in isolated pockets in Madhya Pradesh, Maharashtra, Bihar, Kerala and Tamil Nadu. In the North-east it is generally known as *jhum*. Various groups of people however, have their own nomenclatures for it.

In India, at present more than 4 million hectares of land has been reported to be covered under swiddening ; and around 6 lakh tribal families are practising this type of cultivation over a million hectares annually.

Despite the fact that in the practice of *jhum* cultivation there is optimal utilisation of natural resources, the forces of modernisation and the process of fast change; and an acute pressure of increased population have brought to relief the relative inefficiency of this form of agriculture. Besides low productivity, this system has been held responsible for disturbing ecological balance by causing disproportionate deforestation. This in turn has been causing huge soil erosion in the areas where this system is in practice. Soil erosion due to water flow, constant high velocity winds and shifting cultivation, extensively practised by the tribal population in the North-east has been a major cause of worry.

Taking into consideration the adverse effects of shifting cultivation, the Government of India and the concerned State Governments have embarked upon a good number of schemes in the successive Five Year Plans to regulate and control the practice in the highly affected areas of the country.

The *Integrated Jhumiya Development Programme* (IJDP) is such an attempt to wean the Jhumias away from the practice of shifting cultivation in the two Autonomous Districts of Karbi Anglong and North Cachar Hills in Assam by providing them with alternative means of livelihood.

By taking require to intensive field investigation ; and on the basis of relevant secondary data, Dr. Das, in the present study makes a sincere attempt to highlight the salient features of the programme as well as to have an empirical assessment of the overall impact of the project on a major hill tribe, namely, the Karbis, inhabiting Karbi Anglong district, Assam.

In the process, he has also very relevantly provided a few suggestions for being considered by the concerned authorities while formulating and implementing various *jhum* control programmes.

In the study, the author has very meticulously taken into consideration all possible parameters like ecology, economy, technology of production and socio-cultural milieu of the *jhum* practitioners to make the understanding a holistic one.

I am confident, the publication will be useful not only for the social scientists, but also for social workers, voluntary agencies, development administrators and educators, planners and all others, concerned with the welfare of our socio-economically backward tribal brethren. The book will be of interest to the general readers as well.

(R.K.Kar)

Professor
Department of Anthropology
Dibrugarh University
Dibrugarh-786 004
ASSAM.

PREFACE

Swidden cultivation, commonly referred to as *jhum* in North-east India is a very primitive method of food production which evolved after the food-gathering stage of human civilisation. Significantly, it is still in existence among the people living in tropical and sub-tropical regions of the world. However, recent studies conducted by distinguished scholars, expert committees and other authorities reveal that at present, such an age-old practice has a relatively more detrimental impact on the economy and the surrounding environment than its beneficial aspects.

Taking into consideration the adverse effects of swidden cultivation, the Government of India and the concerned State Governments have embarked upon a good number of schemes under the different Five Year Plans to regulate and control the practice in the highly affected areas of the country.

The *Integrated Jhumia Development Programme* (IJDP) is such an attempt to wean the *jhumias* away from the practice of shifting cultivation in the two autonomous districts of Karbi Anglong and North Cachar Hills of Assam by providing them with alternative permanent means of livelihood. The present study intends to highlight every aspect of the programme in detail and tries to assess the overall impact of the programme on a major hill tribe viz., the Karbis, inhabiting the Karbi Anglong district of the State of Assam. As a matter of fact, the study was undertaken by me for my doctoral research at the Dibrugarh University.

The study now brought out in a book form has been possible due to constant help and active co-operation received from various individuals and organisations at different periods of time. At the very outset, I would like to express my deep sense of gratitude to my guide, Dr. R.K. Kar, Professor, Department of Anthropology, Dibrugarh University, Assam who has supervised the entire study with minute details in spite of his busy schedule of work. He has been, in fact, a source of inspiration and a guiding spirit in my endeavour.

I record my indebtedness to Late Dr. B.N. Bordoloi, former Director, Assam Institute of Research for Tribals and Scheduled Castes, Guwahati who has instilled the idea of research activities in the most interior and in hospitable tribal areas of the two autonomous hill districts of Assam since the beginning of my professional career.

While collecting relevant data in relation to my study, I received immense help from the Project Co-ordinator, IJDP, Office of the Development Commissioner, Hill Areas of Assam, Dispur; Project Officers (IJDP) of both the Karbi Anglong Autonomous Council, Diphu and North Cachar Hills Autonomous Council, Haflong and a good number of officials of other Development Departments located in the two hill districts of Assam. I offer my sincerest thanks to all of them.

During my field visits the people of all the IJDP Centres have extended full co-operation including hospitality without which the dream of completing the present task would not have been fulfilled. I owe my indebtedness to them.

Shri Sing Kro, B.A., an employee of the District Primary Education Programme (DPEP), Karbi Anglong has helped me with great enthusiasm in various stages of the work including field trips to the centres. I offer my thanks to him.

I acknowledge with thanks the help and co-operation extended by Shri Purnananda Bharali, M.A., District Research Officer, Dibrugarh; Late Ananda Chandra Nath, M.Sc., Shri Sanjib Tarafdar, B.Lib. Sc., Shri Samir Choudhury and Shri Tarini Kalita, all from the Directorate of AIRTSC, Guwahati ; Shri Bishnu Prasad Handique, M.Sc., Govt. Boys' Higher Secondary School, Diphu ; Shri Deba Gogoi, Office of the Deputy Commissioner, Karbi Anglong, Diphu and Shri Siba Nath Sarmah, Late Jogen Kalita and Shri Dilip Kumar Brahma of my own establishment, in a number of ways at different phases of the work.

I am deeply indebted to my father, Shri Santopal Das, who is a constant source of inspiration for me not only in this endeavour but also in every sphere of my life. My wife Chitralekha, daughter Rijumani and son Biswajit deserve appreciation for their encouragement in early completion of the work.

Last but not least, I am thankful to Mr. M.P. Misra, Director, Akansha Publishing House, New Delhi for publishing the book within a very short period.

In fine, I would once again like to put on record my gratitude to Prof. R.K. Kar for writing the 'Foreword' to the book.

Diphu
Karbi Anglong

Girindra Nath Das

I

INTRODUCTION

The State of Assam endowed with fertile river valleys and green mountains has been the abode of various tribes with rich cultural heritage since remote past. The tribal communities have entered into the State from their original habitats through different routes at different intervals of time and have permanently settled here. Ethnically all the tribes of Assam belong to the great Mongoloid group and linguistically they belong to the Sino-Tibetan group. The tribes of Assam may conveniently be classified into two main categories–the plains tribes and the hill tribes. The plains tribes are exclusively found in the Brahmaputra and Barak valleys of the State. On the other hand, the hill tribes are mainly concentrated in the two autonomous hill districts of Karbi Anglong and North Cachar Hills which are commonly referred to as the Hill Areas of Assam.

The Scheduled Castes and Scheduled Tribes Orders (Amendment) Act, 1976 specifies the following fourteen tribes in the two hill districts of Assam–(1) Chakma (2) Dimasa Kachari (3) Garo (4) Hajong (5) Hmar (6) Khasi, Jaintiya, Synteng, Pnar, War, Bhoi, Lyngngam (7) any Kuki tribe (8) Lakher (9) Man (Tai speaking) (10) any Mizo (Lushai) tribe (11) Mikir (Karbi) (12) any Naga tribe (13) Pawi and (14) Syntheng. Again, according to the same Act, the following nine tribes have been scheduled in the State of Assam, excluding the autonomous districts– (1) Barmans in Cachar (2) Boro, Boro-Kachari (3) Deori (4) Hojai (5) Kachari, Sonowal (6) Lalung (Tiwa) (7) Mech (8) Miri (Mishing) and (9) Rabha. According to 1991 Census the scheduled tribe population constitutes 12.82 per cent of the total population of Assam.

The Karbi Anglong district is inhabited by the Karbis, Bodos, Tiwas, Dimasa Kacharis, Rengma Nagas, Garos, Kukis and Shyams etc., while the

North Cachar Hills district is inhabited by the Dimasa Kacharis, Jeme Nagas, Hmars, Kukis, Mizos, Karbis and Khasis etc. As a matter of fact, the major concentration of the Karbis is found in the Karbi Anglong district. On the other hand, the North Cachar Hills district is predominantly inhabited by the Dimasa Kacharis.

According to 1991 Census the autonomous hill districts of Assam i.e. Karbi Anglong and North Cachar Hills together cover a total geographical area of 15,322 sq. km. out of the State's total area of 78,438 sq. km. The total population of the two districts is found to be 8,13,524 against the State's total population of 2,24,14,322. In other words, the two hill districts cover 19.5% of the total geographical area and 3.6% of the total population of the State.

The Karbi Anglong district located between latitudes 25°30′ and 26°41′ N and longitudes 92°7′ and 93°52′ E is bounded on the north by Nagaon and Golaghat districts, on the south by the North Cachar Hills district, on the east by Golaghat district and Nagaland and on the west by Meghalaya. The district happens to be the largest district in the State covering a total geographical area of 10,434 sq. km. as per 1991 Census. The total population of the district is 6,62,723. On the whole, the district covers 13.3% and 2.95% of the State's total area and total population respectively. Physiographically, the district consists of two hilly lobes which genetically belong to the Shillong plateau. The two lobes are separated by the Kopili valley. The eastern lobe is dome shaped and approximately double the size of the western lobe. The important rivers of the district are Kopili and Dhansiri. The tributaries of Kopili are Barapani, Umium, Amreng, Kolonga and Jamuna etc., while those of Dhansiri are Kaliani, Nambar, Deopani and Doigrung etc. The highest peak in the district is the Singhason (1357 metres) located at East Karbi Anglong.

The district of North Cachar Hills lies between latitudes 25° and 25°45′ N and longitudes 92°30′ and 93°30′ E. It is bounded by Karbi Anglong and Nagaon districts on the north, Cachar district on the south, Nagaland and Manipur on the east and Meghalaya on the west. The district with a total geographical area of 4,888 sq. km. covers a total population of 1,50,801, thus having 6.2% and 0.67% of the State's total area and total population respectively. The northern flanks of the Barail range and the eastern flanks of the Jayantia hills constitute the North Cachar Hills. The highest peak Hempeupet (1571 metres) is located at the Barail range. Diyung is the longest river (170 km.) of the district. Orignating from the Barail range it flows to join Kopili at Diyungmukh. The tributaries of this river are Langting, Lumding and Mahur etc. Again, Jatinga, Jiri and Chiri, rising from the North Cachar Hills become the tributaries of Barak, the principal river of the Cachar district of Assam.

It may be mentioned here that the two hill districts were, in fact, two subdivisions of the United Mikir & North Cachar Hills district which was inaugurated on November 17, 1951 and created (vide Govt. Notification No. TAD/R 31/503/209 dated 3.11.50) by carving out certain portions of Nagaon, erstwhile Sibsagar and United Khasi and Jayantia Hills districts and the whole of the North Cachar subdivision of Cachar district. On February 2, 1970 North Cachar was declared as a separate civil district while the remaining portion, i.e. Mikir Hills subdivision was constituted into Mikir Hills district which was again rechristened as Karbi Anglong in 1976 vide Govt. Notification No. TAD/R/115/74/47 dated 14.10.76.

In accordance with the provisions of the Sixth Schedule to the Constitution of India, the North Cachar Hills District Council and the Karbi Anglong (Mikir Hills) District Council came into existence on April 20 and June 23, 1952 respectively. The powers and functions of the District Councils may be broadly divided into four heads–Legislative, Executive, Financial and Judicial. Each council has a tenure of five years. The District Council budget consists of two sections–Council Sector and State Sector. The Council Sector budget is entirely dependent upon the revenue collected through the Taxation Department of the Council while the State Sector is financed jointly by the Centre and the Government of Assam.

The Karbi Anglong district has three civil subdivisions viz., Diphu, Hamren and Bokajan while the North Cachar Hills district has two civil subdivisions viz., Haflong and Maibang. It may be noted here that Bokajan and Maibang subdivisions have come into existence on August 15, 1989 and November 17, 1987 respectively. Again, there are 4 Revenue Circles, namely; Phulani, Diphu, Silanijan and Donka in Karbi Anglong and 3 Revenue Circles, namely; Haflong, Maibang and Harangajao in North Cachar Hills. Moreover, the number of Development Blocks is 10 and 4 in Karbi Anglong and North Cachar Hills respectively. Some basic statistics in relation to the two autonomous hill districts of Assam are furnished in Table I.1 as per 1991 Census. The table shows that as per 1991 Census the scheduled tribe population in Karbi Anglong accounts for 51.56% of the total population of the district whereas in respect of North Cachar Hills it accounts for 65.54% of the total population of the district. On the contrary, the records of 1971 Census reveal that the scheduled tribe populations numbering 2,10,039 in Karbi Anglong and 52, 583 in North Cachar Hills constitute 55.37% and 69.14% of the total population of Karbi Anglong and North Cachar Hills respectively. The tribewise population figures in the two districts as per 1991 Census are still not available. Nevertheless, to have an idea of the same, 1971 figures have been presented in Table I.2. It will be seen from the table that among the various tribal communities inhabiting the two districts the Karbis are predominant in Karbi Anglong and Dimasa Kacharis are predominant in North Cachar Hills. In fact, the Karbis and Dimasa Kacharis constitute 82.29% and 46.68% of the total scheduled tribe population of Karbi Anglong and North Cachar Hills respectively.

The main source of livelihood of the tribal people inhabiting the two hill districts of Assam is agriculture. The people carry out wet cultivation in the low lying areas. But they practise *jhum* or shifting cultivation in an extensive manner on the hill slopes.

Shifting Cultivation in General

Shifting cultivation is the most primitive method of cultivation and its evolution is supposed to take place during the neolithic period. "It is known through archaeological discoveries that by about 7000 B.C., there was a fundamental change in man's attitude towards environment and accidentally he became a food producer from a hunter and food gatherer. Man began to plant, cultivate and improve species of various plants by selection. Of course, domestication of animals like sheep, goat and cattle started side by side. Goardon Childe identified the neolithic farmers of the Danube Valley as nomadic cultivators. Chang also proved that the neolithic farmers of Formosa were shifting cultivators" (Bose, Ghatak & Bera, 1982 : 216).

Shifting cultivation has been defined as "any agricultural system in which fields are cleared by firing and are cropped discontinuously (implying periods of fallowing which is always in average longer than periods of cropping)" (Conklin, 1957 : 1). "The chief characteristic features of shifting cultivation are (i) rotation of fields (ii) slash and burn operation of vegetable species (iii) keeping the land fallow for a number of years for regeneration of forests (iv) use of human labour as chief input (v) non-employment of

TABLE I. 1
Basic statistics in relation to the two hill districts of Assam (1991 Census)

Sl. No.	*Item*	*Karbi Anglong*	*North Cachar Hills*
1	*2*	*3*	*4*
1	Geographical Area (sq. km.)	10,434	4,888
2	Subdivision	3	2
3	Total population	6,62,723	1,50,801
	Male	3,47,607 (52.45)	81,196 (53.84)
	Female	3,15,116 (47.55)	69,605 (46.16)
4	Total ST population	3,41,718 (51.56)	98,834 (65.54)
	Male	1,75,289 (51.30)	51,064 (51.67)
	Female	1,66,429 (48.70)	47,770 (48.33)
5	Total SC population	27,991 (4.22)	3,918 (2.60)
	Male	14,879 (53.16)	2,312 (59.01)
	Female	13,112 (46.84)	1,606 (40.99)
6	Total rural population	5,92,257 (89.37)	1,16,315 (77.13)
	Male	3,08,543 (52.10)	61,870 (53.19)
	Female	2,83,714 (47.90)	54.445 (46.81)

continued ....

TABLE I.1
Basic statistics in relation to the two hill districts of Assam (1991 Census)

1	*2*	*3*	*4*
7	Total urban population	70,466 (10.63)	34,486 (22.87)
	Male	39,064 (55.44)	19,326 (56.04)
	Female	31,402 (44.56)	15,160 (43.96)
8	Total main workers	2,52,123 (38.04)	57,751 (38.30)
9	Percentage of literacy (including 0-6 year age group)	35.88	46.58
	Male	44.15	54.39
	Female	26.76	37.46
10	Density of population per sq. km.	64	31
11	Sex Ratio (Females per 1000 males)	907	857
12	Growth rate of population (1971-91)	+ 74.72	+ 98.30

(*Source* : *Statistical Hand Book*, Assam, 1984, Directorate of Economics & Statistics, Government of Assam, Guwahati)

N.B. : Figures shown in parentheses indicate percentages.

TABLE I.2
Scheduled Tribe population in the two hill districts of Assam (1971 Census)

Sl. No.	*Name of the tribe*	*Karbi Anglong*	*North Cachar Hills*
1	*2*	*3*	*4*
1	Mikir (Karbi)	1,72,845	4,349
2	Dimasa (Kachari)	14,797	24,545
3	Garo	9,080	59
4	Khasi & Jayantia	4,763	1,724
5	Chakma	246	150
6	Hajong	384	2
7	Hmar	13	5,367
8	Any Kuki tribe	5,937	7,587
9	Lakher	–	1
10	Man (Tai speaking)	964	–
11	Any Mizo (Lushai) tribe	347	364
12	Any Naga tribe	46	8,435
13	Pawi	6	–
14	Synteng	611	–
	Total	2,10,039	52,583

(Source : *Statistical Hand Book,* Assam, 1980, Directorate of Economics & Statistics, Government of Assam, Guwahati)

draught animal and (vi) use of simple implements like dibble stick, scrapper etc" (Roy Burman, 1989 : 1).

The practice of shifting cultivation is observed in the tropical and sub-tropical parts of the world. Besides India, it is found in Srilanka, Northern Burma, Thailand, Sumatra, Borneo, Indonesia, Philippines, Korea, Guatemala, Amazon, Madagascar, Keniya, Ivory Coast and New Guinea etc. In India, it is prevalent in the States of Assam, Meghalaya, Nagaland, Mizoram, Arunachal Pradesh, Manipur, Tripura, Bihar, Orissa, Madhya Pradesh, Sikkim, Andhra Pradesh, Karnataka, Kerala, Tamil Nadu, Rajasthan, Gujarat and Maharashtra. However, the practice of shifting cultivation has posed a serious problem in Orissa, Andhra Pradesh and North-east India.

The procedure of carrying out this type of cultivation is that a suitable plot of land on a hill slope is selected and the trees, bamboos and shrubs etc., grown over it are cut in the winter season and these are allowed to dry under the blazing summer sun. Later on, fire is set on the debris and the ashes, thus produced, are scattered over the whole plot of land. With the advent of monsoon rain, seeds of paddy, maize and cotton etc., are broadcast over the area. Seeds of some other crops and vegetables are also put into the holes made by digging stick or other implements. Thus, mixed crop is raised over the same plot of land. Weeding also takes place. As soon as crops ripe, harvesting starts. Vidyarthi (1986 : 87) mentions the following thirteen stages adopted by the shifting cultivators: (i) selecting the forest patch or land (ii) worshipping (iii) cutting the forest growth and spreading it' for drying (iv) collecting big logs and firewood (v) setting fire to the shrubs (vi) planning or final preparation of the field for sowing (vii) sowing seeds with digging sticks or with the help of hoes (viii) weeding (ix) watching and protecting the crop (x) harvesting and storing (xi) worshipping (xii) merry-making and (xiii) fallowing.

In the North-eastern States of India shifting cultivation is commonly known as *jhum*. The cultivators practising this cultivation are called *Jhumia*. The term *Jhum* prevalent in the North-eastern region of India has most probably evolved from China. "China was known in old days by a general term *Chao-Thieus*, meaning God's Heaven-land, and even to this day, the people of northern Burma designate China by the general term *Thieus*. *Chao-Thieus* was later on shortened to *Chuh-This*, and was also pronounced as *Zuh-This*. *Chao*, *Chuh* or *Zuh* later on meant only high hill or high land. Cultivation carried on by picking up a high hill or high land was known as *Zuh-moh* or *Zuhm* cultivation" (Nath, 1978 : 1).

The most important features of *jhum* cultivation in North-east India are–(a) Land is owned by the community but each family cultivates its own field after selecting the same jointly with the help of headman. (b) Fire is employed to clear the cut and dried up debris. *Jhuming* is not done without burning–if no fire is employed as in many other parts of India and abroad––then it is believed that the process causes relatively less damage to ecology. (c) Soil is not cultivated. (d) Community approach in certain broad operations–jungle clearance, burning crop, protection from animals. (e) Yield goes down rapidly–hence field is abandoned after 2-3 years. (f) The field remains with the *jhumia* as long as he continues to use it (Goswami, 1994 : 9).

Local names for *jhum* are prevalent among the peoples of the world. "The primitive cultivators of West Africa call it *farming* and it is known as *sartage* in the Ardennes, *chena* in Srilanka, *chitamoni* in Central Africa, *nutpa* in Central America, *karen* in Japan, *ladeng* in Indonesia, *djuma* in Sumatra and *tamari* in Thailand" (Agarwal, 1987 : 317). "*Jhum* cultivation goes under a variety of names in other parts of India : *Kurwa* or *Khallu* in the Santhal Parganas, *Bewara* in Ranchi and *Palamau* in Bihar and *Podu*, *Rema*, *Dahi*, *Kaman*, *Bringa*, *Gudia*, *Dongar Chas* in Orissa; *Penda*, *Dahiya*, *Bewar*, *Guharh*, *Farhha*, *Dippa*, *Marhan*, or *Erka* in Madhya Pradesh ; and *Kondapady* in Andhra Pradesh" (Vidyarthi, 1986 : 86). In North-east India some of the local names go as; *Hichusisomoms* among the Reangs of Tripura, *Adimdik* among the Adis of Arunachal Pradesh, *Lyngkhalum* or *Shyrti* among the Khasis, *Bogma* among the Garos of Meghalaya, *Tekeonglu* among the Ao Nagas of Nagaland and *Inglong Arit* among the Karbis of Assam etc.

The precise statistical data on the extent of shifting cultivation in the world are not available. "According to F.A.O's estimate (in the 4th World Forestry Congress) the actual area under shifting cultivation in the world was reported to be about 36 million sq. km. inhabited by some 200 million people" (Vidyarthi, 1986 : 86). In India, according to Kaith (1956) the total area of land utilized for shifting cultivation is 13,55,300 acres and the total tribal population dependent upon it is around 26,44,200 belonging to 109 tribal communities (Sachchidananda, 1989 : 22). According to Roy

Burman and Sharma (1970) the total area under shifting cultivation and the total population depending on it in India as per 1961 estimates are 18,42,816 acres and 18,10,400 individuals respectively (Sachchidananda, 1989 : 33). As per Dhebar Commission Report (1962), the total area under shifting cultivation in India is about 5,60,000 hectares (14 lakh acres). According to the Report of the Commissioner for Scheduled Castes and Scheduled Tribes (1961), the total area of land under shifting cultivation in India is 22,75,616 acres and the total population depending on it is approximately 25,89,401 (Bose, Ghatak & Bera, 1982 : 226). Shifting cultivation is being carried out in about 233 blocks located in 62 districts of 16 States of the country. It involves about 12% of the total tribal population of the country (Roy Burman, 1982). However, the total number of families engaged in this practice in India as shown in an article by Borthakur (1991 : 89) is furnished in Table I.3. The table reveals that among the thirteen States and two Union Territories (at present States) in India practising shifting cultvation, the total number of families engaged in this type of cultivation is highest in Orissa and lowest in Madhya Pradesh. Again, in North-east India the number of households engaged in *jhum* is maximum in Nagaland and minimum in Tripura.

The Task Force Report on shifting cultivation, Ministry of Agriculture, 1983 shows the extent of the practice in North-east Region of India, an idea of which is provided in Table I.4. The table shows that the annual area under shifting cultivation is highest in Manipur and lowest in Nagaland. Fallow period varies from 2-10 years in the region. Minimum area under shifting cultivation at one time or other is maximum in Manipur and minimum in Tripura.

From the discussions made so far it is not known clearly whether the practice of shifting cultivation is increasing or decreasing in India. However, as per estimates of 1960-61 and 1974-75 (Table I.5), "the area under shifting cultivation and population dependent on it have gone up in all the units in the North-east and Orissa. In other States it has either declined or disappeared" (Kar, 1986 : 41).

Studies conducted by various authorities reveal that the population sustaining capacity of land under shifting cultivation is extremely low. "The studies conducted in the Philippines, Malawi and Zambia including a few in India (*eg*. Bose, 1967; Ganguli, 1969 & Saha, 1970) reveal the same. For example, the estimate of Bose's study noted slightly over four persons

TABLE I.3
Number of families engaged in shifting cultivation

Sl. No.	*State/Union Territories*	*Total number of families engaged in jhuming*
1	*2*	*3*
	A. STATE	
1	Andhra Pradesh	23,200 (A)
2	Assam	58,000 (A)
3	Bihar	12,200 (A)
4	Madhya Pradesh	2,500 (A)
5	Manipur	70,000 (A)
6	Meghalaya	52,290 (A)
7	Nagaland	1,16,046 (A)
8	Orissa	1,41,000 (A)
9	Tripura	43,000 (A)
10	Sikkim	3,000 (B)
11	Karnataka	2,800 (B)
12	Maharashtra	5,000 (B)
13	Kerala	3,200 (B)
	B. UNION TERRITORY (at present State)	
1	Arunachal Pradesh	54,000 (A)
2	Mizoram	50,000 (A)
	Total	6,36,236

A–Based on Task Force on *Shifting Cultivation in India*, October, 1983.

B–Figures are approximate and based on FAO UNFPA Project 1980 (Report for India–*Population data regarding Forestry communities practising shifting cultivation and other Reports, 1992).*

TABLE I.4
Shifting cultivation in North–east Region

Sl. No.	*State*	*Annual area under shifting cultivation (sq. km)*	*Fallow period (in yrs)*	*Minimum area under shifting cultivation at one time or other (sq. km)*	*Number of families practising shifting cultivation*
1		*2*	*3*	*4*	*5*
1	Arunachal Pradesh	700	3-10	2,100	54,000
2	Assam	696	2-10	1,392	58,000
3	Manipur	900	4-7	3,600	70,000
4	Meghalaya	530	5-7	2,650	52,290
5	Mizoram	630	3-4	1,890	50,000
6	Nagaland	190	5-8	1,913	1,16,046
7	Tripura	223	5-9	1,115	43,000
	Total	3,869 (1.5%)		14,660 (5.7%)	4,43,336

Source: *Basic Statistics of North–Eastern Region*, 1990 North–Eastern Council, Shillong.

TABLE I.5

Estimated area under shifting cultivation, communities and population depending on shifting cultivation (a) 1960-61 & (b) 1974-75

Sl. No.	*State*	*District(s) affected*	*Tribes practising it*	**Estimated area under shifting cultivation for a year (sq. km)*	**Estimated population partially depended on shifting cultivation (thousand)*
1	*2*	*3*	*4*	*5*	*6*
1	Andhra	(a)Srikakulam, Agency tracts, Visakhapattnam, East Godabari, and West Godabari	Bagata, Gadabas, Kammara, Khonds, Kotiyas, Koyas, Konda–Reddis, Konda–Dhors, Malis, Manna–Dhors, Nayaks, Rena Saṿarms	384	200
		(b)East Godabari, Srikakulam and Vizag	Bagata, Jataus, Konda–Dhors, Konda Kapus, Konda–Reddis, Mukha Dhara, Samantha, Savaras	173	116
2	Arunachal Pradesh	(a)Not available		600*	500*

Contd.

1	2	3	4	5	6
		(b) Kameng, Lohit, Siang, Subansiri & Tirap	Adi including the sub-groups of Gallong, Miniyong, Padam, Pasi Ashing, Bagni, Bagum, Simong and Tangam Aka, Dafla or Nishi, Hill Miri, Khowa, Mishimi, Miji, Nocte, Tangsa and Wancho	920	797
3	Assam, Meghalaya, Nagaland, Mizoram	(a) Garo Hills, United Mikir & N.C.Hills, United Khasi & Jaintia Hills, Naga Hills, Mizo (Lushai) Hills Kamrup, Nowgong, Cachar	Chakma, Garo, Jaintia, Khasi, Lushai, Lalung, Mikir, Mizo, Naga	2035	977
	Assam	(b) Karbi Anglong & N.C. Hills	Dimasa (Kachari), Garo, Kachari, Karbi or Mikir, Khasi, Kuki, Lalung & Naga	690	331

Contd.

1	2	3	4	5	6
	Meghalaya	(b) West Garo Hills, East Garo Hills, East Khasi Hills, Jaintia Hills & West Khasi Hills	Garo, Hmar, Jaintia, Khasi & Mikir	760	344
	Nagaland	(b) Khoma, Phek, Mokekchung, Mon Tuensang, Wokha & Zunhebote	Nagar, Kuki & Mikir	730	396
	Mizoram	(b) Aizawal, Chhimutuipul and Lunglei districts	Chakma, Hmar, Lakher, Mizo, Pawri & Riang	650	295
4	Bihar	(a) Singbhum Santal Parganas, Ranchi	Birija, Kharis, Norwas Mal Paharias, Sarria Paharia	436	115
		(b) Santal Parganas	Mal Paharia & Sauria Paharia	162	61
5	Karnataka	(a) Interior Mountainous tracts of Belgaum and South Kanara district	Bettakurba, Jenu Kurubam, Kumbis, Kuman Marat. Soligars	10	14
		(b) Not availabale			

Contd.

1	2	3	4	5	6
6	Kerala	(a) Attappady, Amosn, Valluvanad Taluk, Malabar district	Irular, Kurumbas, Kurichains Mudugar, Paniyan	40	10
		(b) Palghat	Kurumbas and Mudugar	19	16
7	Gujarat				
	Maharashtra	(a) Dang dist. and in some parts of Surat dist., Kelaba dist., South Chanda Division, Janjira subdivision	Bhil, Kumbi, Kakanis Mavcai Varhli Halkki Kethari Kumari, Maratha Maria Gond, Thakur, Wakhals	298	25
		(b) Not available			
8	Madhya Pardesh	(a) Durg, Bastar, Chhindwara, Chanda, Balaghat, Nandia, Raigarh	Agariya, Baiga Bharia, Gond, Korva, Kodaku, Madia, Majhwar, Mawasi	90	30
		(b) Bastar	Hill Maria	81	15
9	Manipur	(a) Hill areas	Angami, Kabui Kacha Naga, Mariang, Tangkhul	216	183

Contd.

1	2	3	4	5	6
		(b) East Dist, North Dist., South dist., Tangnopal & West District	Anal, Chothe, Hmar, Kabui, Kacha Naga, Lamgang, Mao Maring, Paite, Simte, Tangkhul, Thadou, Vaiphui and Zou	600	293
10	Orissa	(a) Keonjhar, Sundergarh, Denkanal, Sambalpur, Kalahandi, Ganjam, Koraput	Bhuiya or Bhuyan, Bhunkia Gadaba, Jatapu, Juang, Koya, Khonda, Kotia Poroja, Saora	1600	937
		(b) Baudh-Khonsmals, Dhenkanel, Ganjam, Keonjhar, Kharagpur, Sundergarh	Shuiya Bondo Proaja, Didayi, Kaluhanoi, Sambalpur	2298	706
11	Tamil Nadu	(a) Coimbatore district, Nilgiri district	Kadar, Kurumbas, Malasar, Pulayans Paniyans	12	22
		(b) Not available			

Contd.

1	2	3	4	5	6
12	Tripura	(a) Sadar, Khowai, Kailashahar, Kamalpur, Dharmanagar, Udaipur, Sonemura. Belonia and Amarpur subdivision	Chakma, Garo, Halam. Jamatia, Kuki, Lushai, Mog, Noatia, Reang, Tripuri	467	196
		(b) North Dist., South Dist. and West District	Chakma, Halam, Jamatia, Lushai, Mag, Noatia, Reang and Tripuri	620	246
	Total (a)			6184	3309
	(b)			13263	3606

* Figures for Arunachal for 1960-61 interpolated by the author for comparison purposes.

Source: 1. Shifting Cultivation in North-East India, published by North-East India Council for Social Science Research, 1976.
2. Report on population Data regarding forestry communities practising shifting cultivation in India (UFA/UNEPA project)

N.B. : The table is reproduced from Kar (1986 : 54)

per square kilometre (Kondakata in Abujhmar Hills, M.P.) to 16 persons per square kilometre (Mamphui village in Mizoram). According to Ganguli, the population sustaining capacity of land under shifting cultivation is noted as six persons per sq.km supposing 50% of the areas amenable to the shifting cultivation. Saha's studies (in Mikir Hills and Mizo Hills) estimate the capacity to be between three to nine persons per sq. km. provided 50% of the area is available for shifting cultivation. It is clear enough that a wide gap remains between the food grains production under shifting cultivation and the population dependent on it. The future gap will be wider still" (Jha, 1988 : 24).

While dealing with the carrying capacity of land under shifting cultivation Majumdar (1990 : 28) refers to these factors: 1. Cultivating factor (i.e. length of the fallow period). 2. Nature of the crops produced (i.e. proportion between crops produced for domestic consumption and crops produced for sale). 3. Standard of living of the population dependent on shifting cultivation. Citing examples from Meghalaya in respect of paddy yields, Majumdar (1990 : 28) opines, "in Meghalaya yield of paddy in shifting cultivation is 461 kg/ha. and if we take the average size of a holding under shifting cultivation as 0.50 ha utilized by a family of 5 members, we find that per capita production of paddy is as low as 46 kg per year which is sufficient for one person barely for three months. From all the factors noted above, it is proved beyond doubt that shifting cultivation has been uneconomic in most of the areas even for people with a very low standard of living. To counteract this, provided they do not have any other alternative, the only way left to the shifting cultivators is to take larger and larger plots by more and more shortening of the fallow period. This only enhances the destruction of forests and consequent evil of soil erosion and ancilliary maladies".

In ancient times the *jhum* cycles were of longer duration due to low density of population. As a result, the land could recuperate its lost fertility. At present, the cycles have become shorter and shorter due to increase of population. Therefore, the land cannot recuperate its lost fertility and the production from the *jhum* fields decreases. The fallow period in respect of shifting cultivation in the North-eastern States has already been furnished in Table I.4. "Theoretically, zones having good soil, high temperature, high rainfall and gentle slope should require less time for completing the regeneration of forests. But whenever land-man ratio is disturbed, people disregard conventional rules by many adjustments, one of which is 'reducing the cycle of regeneration'. The Hill Maria of Abhujmar Hills can wait for 16 years for regeneration of forests because of their low density of population. On the contrary, though there is not so much ecological variation, Juang of Keonjhar due to their high density of population cannot wait for 10-12 years for regeneration. The same is true for Ganjam, Srikakulam, Koraput and Visakhapatnam districts also" (Bose, Ghatak & Bera, 1982 : 219). Moreover, shifting cultivation leads to soil erosion, silting up of river beds causing devastating floods in the plains, destruction of forest wealth and ecological imbalance etc. "Shifting cultivation which is practised in the North-eastern region has proved to be a menace. Besides decline in economic yield, the system has resulted into a series of serious environmental problems. There has been altercation in species composition and large scale invasion of exotic weeds. Local climate-species have got eliminated from *jhum* fields and are confined only to protected forests. Thus, many of them are threatened and endangered" (Boro, 1996).

The traditional ownership pattern of land under shifting cultivation is generally community oriented. "We know that the concept of territorial rights and exclusive command of the community over the resources therein had developed at a very early stage in the history of mankind. This principle has remained more or less inviolable in all communities practising shifting cultivation. The individual has only usufractuary right over the field which he cultivates for a limited period. The most important characteristic feature is, therefore, the community action and participation in the entire economic activity in the relevant area. The social organization of the people is built around the concepts of community worship community participation and commual responsibility" (Kar, op cit. : 46). In this connection it may be mentioned here that some tribes practise the system of private ownership of land. " As for example, among the Zemi Nagas of the North Cachar Hills there are traditional land owners called *kadepeo*. A *kadepeo's* land not only includes *jhum* sites and land suitable for settled cultivation situated in and around the village, but village sites as well. For occupation of land at village sites and for cultivating land at *Jhum* sites the villagers have to pay rent in kind (to him) usually @ 5 kg per annum. There are also lands which are exclusively owned by the six clans of the Zemis. Only the remaining *Jhum* sites are owned by the community" (Bordoloi, 1990 : 240).

It may, however, be emphasized that shifting cultivation has been an integral part of the life and culture of the various tribal communities. As a matter of fact, most of the socio-cultural and religious aspects are intimately connected with this system of cultivation. "Certain social, cultural and even religious functions are associated with certain aspects of agricultural operations in shifting cultivation, e.g. *Agalmaka*, before burning of *Jhum*; *Ahaia*, after harvesting, *Rongchugala*, before harvesting and *Wangala*, after completion of all operations in *Jhum*, are celebrated in Garo Hills. Stephen Tyler (1974) observed that shifting cultivation is not just an alternate form of land use or a set of agricultural practices, but it implies the whole nexus of people's religious belief, attitude, self-image and the tribal identity. In Nagaland, connected with agricultural operations are the *Tsakro*, the old man who begins the sowing operation; and *Lidepfue*, the old woman who helps in reaping the crop. Since several festivities are associated with shifting cultivation, abandoning of the practice would mean leaving these functions and festivals. Agriculture is that sector of human activity in which there is greatest interaction between the environment and the culture which has grown in and from it (Schlippe, 1956). All cultures are intimately linked with the mode of subsistence" (Sharma and Prasad, 1994 : 9).

Shifting Cultivation in Karbi Anglong

The approximate ratio of hills to plains in the district of Karbi Anglong is 60 : 40. The people practise wet cultivation in the plains area. The hills area includes State Reserved Forests, District Council Reserved Forests and the Unclassified Forests. The Unclassified Forests may again be subdivided into hills and low lying forest lands. "While in the hills the tribal people practise *Jhuming*, in the low lying forest lands other types of cultivation are carried on by making the land suitable after proper reclamation. So far as the hills are concerned the tribal people think themselves to be the common owners and the District Council Authority does not interfere with this common ownership. In the low lying forest lands, where people undertake cultivation, they may apply for ownership right to the District Council Authority. If the Authority grants this right of ownership, it is well and good and in case of refusal conflicts develop. The people rather consider it to be an infringement on their rights in the forest" (Bordoloi, 1991 : 207).

The Report of National Commission (NCA) Part IX on Forestry, 1976 reveals that in the Assam Hills, the total area affected by *jhum* is 4,98,000 hectares and area under *jhum* at one time is 69,000 hectares. Again, the total number of tribal families involved in *jhuming* is 58,000. Detailed break-up of the figures in respect of the two hill districts is shown in Table I.6. The table reveals that the total area of land affected by *jhum* is 4,15,000 hectares in Karbi Anglong and 83,000 hectares in North Cachar Hills. The number of tribal families involved in *jhuming* is 45,000 and 13,000 in Karbi Anglong and North Cachar Hills respectively. Again, land utilisation in the two hill districts of Assam during 1978-79 as shown by Barman (1990 : 221) is furnished in Table I.7. The table shows that the total *jhum* area is 21,853 hectares in Karbi Anglong and 6,475 hectares in North Cachar Hills as per Report of Assam Agricultural Commission, 1975. The number of *jhumia* families is 20,000 and 7,000 in Karbi Anglong and N. C. Hills respectively.

According to Bordoloi (1990 : 238) the estimated *jhumia* families in Karbi Anglong district are 23,400 in 1976 on the basis of 1971 Census enumeration. Again, Bhattacharjee (1990 : 234) has estimated the *jhumia* families in the district to be 29,424 in 1979.

In this context it may be mentioned here that the Assam Remote Sensing Application Centre (ASTE Council) has carried out a satellite survey of shifting cultivation in the Assam hills. It indicates that "the practice of *jhuming* in the two hill districts of Assam has been widespread and is intensifying in the recent years. The study is carried out for two different time periods viz., 1986-87 and 1993-94 using the data from the satellite IRS-IB (LISS II) and Landsat (TM) on 1 : 50,000 scale. It reveals that in the Karbi Anglong district the current area under *jhum* has increased from 13,583 hectares (1.302 per cent of total geographical area) in 1986-87 to 69,125 hectares (6.625 per cent of total geographical area) in 1993-94. The corresponding figures for the N.C. Hills district are 22,807 hectares (4.67 per cent of geographical area) and 69,447 hectares (14.21 per cent of geographical area) in 1986-87 and 1993-94 respectively. With regard to the abandoned *jhum* areas of 1-5 years cycle covered with scrubs or grasses, the figures for Karbi Anglong district are 26,367 ha (2.52 p.c. of geographical area) for 1986-87 and 39,661 ha (3.8 p.c. of geographical area) for 1993-94. In N.C. Hills the increase from 65,682 hectares (13.44 per cent) in 1986-87 to 71,023 hectares (14.53 per cent) in 1993-94 is observed. Evergreen and semi ever green forests in the Karbi Anglong district has been reduced from 27.64 per cent in 1986-87 to 22.9 per cent in 1993-94. The corresponding figures for the N.C. Hills district are 26.78 per cent and 18.975 per cent respectively. Deciduous forests (*Sal* and Teak) also show

TABLE I.6

Jhuming in the Assam Hills and the number of Tribal Famillies involved (1976)

Sl. No.	*Name of the district*	*Area affected by jhum (000 ha)*	*Area under jhum at one time (000 ha)*	*No. of tribal families involved (000)*
1	*2*	*3*	*4*	*5*
1	Karbi Anglong (Mikir Hills)	415	54	45
2	North Cachar Hills	83	15	13
	Total	498	69	58

TABLE I.7

Land utilisation in the Assam Hills during 1978-79 (Area in hectare)

Sl. No.	*Item*	*Karbi Anglong*	*North Cachar Hills*
1	*2*	*3*	*4*
1	Geographical Area	10,33,200	4,48,000
2	Area under forest	2,73,514 (26.5)	63,339 (12.9)
3	Barren & unculturable land	6,33,032 (61.3)	4,04,975 (82.8)
4	Net area shown	1,26,654 (12.2)	20,686 (4.3)
5	Total cropped area	1,45,559 (14.1)	22,186 (4.5)
6	Area sown more than once	18,945 (13)	1,500 (6.5)
7	*Jhum* area*	21,853	6,475
8	*Jhum* area as per cent of net area shown	17	29
9	No. of *Jhumia* families*	20,000	7,000

*Figures furnished by respective District Councils quoted in the *Report of Assam Agricultural Commission,* (1975), Govt. of Assam, pp 143-44.

Source : Directorate of Economics and Statistics, Govt. of Assam, Guwahati.

Note : Figures shown in the brackets indicate the percentage of the total geographical areas of the respective districts.The percentages in Sl. No. 6 is calculated out of the figures in Sl. No. 5.

N.B. : The table is reproduced from Barman (1990 : 221).

a decrease from 8122 hectares in 1986-87 to 5251 hectares in 1993-94 in the Karbi Anglong district as against 17,310 hectares in 1986-87 and 10,371 hectares in 1993-94 in N.C. Hills district. Pure bamboo strands also showed a decline in Karbi Anglong district from 12,192 hectares (11.67 per cent of geographical area) in 1986-87 to 10,562 hectares (10.012 per cent of geographical area) in 1993-94 as against 81,704 hectares (16.72 per cent of geographical area) in 1986-87 to 63,542 hectares (13 percent of geographical area) in 1993-94 in the N.C. Hills district. For mixed bamboo the figures are 4,65,296 hectares (44.59 per cent) in 1986-87 as against 3,48,882 hectares (33.43 per cent) in 1993-94 in Karbi Anglong district and corresponding figures for N.C. Hills district are 93,680 hectares (19.16 per cent) in 1986-87 and 78,932 hectares (16.14 per cent) in 1993-94 respectively. The study also indicates considerable increase in the scrub land due to loss of soil fertility as a result of *jhuming* and degradation of forest areas. The total area affected by *jhum* cultivation (including current *jhum*, abandoned *jhum*, mixed bamboo and scrub land) has increased from 56.95 per cent to 60.10 percent in Karbi Anglong district and 46.51 percent to 56.18 percent in N.C. Hills district respectively. This clearly indicates intensification of *jhuming* practice in the Assam Hills" (*The Assam Tribune*, 1996).

From the foregoing discussion it may be said that although various authorities have provided statistical data relating to *jhum* land and the number of tribal families involved with it in different ways, precise data in connection with *jhum* are not available. It may be mentioned here that preparation of land records by conducting a Cadastral Survey was initiated in the Karbi Anglong district during the Fifth Plan. But all the villages have not yet been covered.

The traditional village council of the Karbis plays an important role in the management of *Jhum* lands. "Among the Karbis it is the village council (*Me*) constituted by the elderly persons and presided over by the Gaonbura (the village headman) which manages the *Jhum* land. The *Me* distributes Jhum land to each family according to its need. Lands in this district have never been managed by tribal chiefs nor are they the virtual owners of the land like the Mizo Chiefs" (*Bordoloi*, 1986 : 130).

The mode of operation of shifting cultivation *(Inglong Arit)* practised by the 'Karbis may be presented in the following manner:

Initially a suitable plot of land is selected on a hill slope in the month of February *(Thang Thang)*. After selecting the plot, the trees, bamboos and other plants and shrubs etc., grown over it are cut and the rubbishes are left for getting dried up under the scorching sun. In the month of April *(Jangmi)* these are burnt to ashes. In the months of May *(Aru)* and June *(Vosik)* the plot of land is made free from the debris and heavy logs, if unburnt are placed aside. Ashes are scattered over the whole area and as soon as rains start, seeds of paddy and some other crops like maize and cotton etc., are broadcast over the ashes. The exercise is associated with the collective singing of lively love songs *(Bongoi Alun)*. Moreover, seeds of various crops and vegetables are put into the holes made by hoe. In fact, the Karbis use to cultivate mixed crop in a plot of land. When the paddy starts growing, they observe *Choklim Kanthur* by worshipping *Longle–A–Hii* Arnam with the hope that wild animals like monkeys and elephants will not destroy paddy fields and the members of the household will not suffer from illness. Generally weeding *(Sok Karlu)* takes place in the month of July *(Jakhong)*. Ahu paddy (*Soksu*) is ready for harvesting in the month of August *(Pai–Pai)*. Again, *Sali* paddy begins to bear cereals in the month of September *(Chiti)* and it is harvested in the month of October *(Phre)*. The paddy thus harvested is stocked in the *jhum* courtyard in the month of November *(Phaikuni)*. Paddy is thrashed in December *(Matijong)* and the thrashed paddy is brought home by the males in basket *(Mantung)* in January *(Arkoi)*. The well-to-do families observe *Sok Keroi Kekan* on the occasion. Girls are not allowed to dance in this festival.

The different stages of *jhum* operations as practised by the Karbis are as follows:

1. *Ritkepan* – The felling of trees and clearing of the undergrowths
2. *Mekekai* – The burning of the debris
3. *Arhikkarhi* – The removal of half-burnt logs
4. *Rik* – Sowing of various types of seeds
5. *Sok Karlu* – Weeding of plants
6. *Sok Kerot* – Harvesting

Tools and implements used for the purpose by the people are very simple. These include spade *(Ku)*, dao *(Nopak)*, sickle *(Nokekrengsu)*, hoe *(Kuso)* and axe *(Chow)* etc. They also use mortar *(Long)* and pestle *(Longpum)* for the purpose of dehusking paddy.

In the past the people shifted their villages frequently in search of *jhum* land. At present, this tendency of shifting the whole village in the neighbourhood of the *jhum* site has been reduced to a great extent.

The period of *jhum* cycle which is a vital factor in productivity has rapidly declined in the district. "In bygone days *jhuming* was not so unproductive as it stands to-day. Because in the past the *jhum* cycles were of longer duration from 10 to 15 years, and hence the land could replenish its lost fertility during this period. But now-a-days owing to increasing pressure of a growing population on land the cycles have become shorter from 4 to 7 years, and as such, it cannot replenish its lost fertility to the soil. Therefore, the yield is also less". (Bordoloi, 1972: 55).

On the basis of a socio-economic survey conducted in a Karbi village, Kanther Terang in the year 1966, Saikia (1968 : 67) comments, "The *jhum* cultivation limits expansion of the village economy. The practice involves great waste in terms of destruction of forests which results in soil erosion. *Jhuming* as a system of farming is highly labour intensive and the output per acre and per worker is extremely low. Such a primitive form of agriculture is not compatible with economic change and development".

Review of Literature on the Studies of Shifting Cultivation

Studies on shifting cultivation have been carried out by various authorities including social scientists, agronomists, forestry experts, soil scientists and ecologists from time to time. A good number of articles on this subject have also come out in the reputed journals, weeklies and research bulletins etc.

So far as the North-eastern region of India is concerned, the Agro-Economic Research Centre for North-east India, Jorhat, the North Eastern Council, Shillong and ICAR Research Complex for NE Hill Region, Shillong have taken keen interest on the study of various aspects of the shifting cultivation.

On the basis of the socio-economic survey of Kanther Terang (a Karbi village in Karbi Anglong) conducted in the year 1960, Ray (1969 : 68) comments, "*Jhuming* or shifting cultivation is of course a much-discussed and, to some extent, a controversial subject. There seems, however, to be no serious difference of opinion about the fact that the practice involves great waste in terms of soil erosion and destruction of forests. Another point, which does not appear to have received so much attention, is that *jhuming* as a system of farming is highly insufficient in the sense that output per acre and output per worker in *jhuming* are both extremely low. This peculiar feature, namely, that of combining a high degree of labour intensity with an even higher degree of land extensiveness, makes the system unsuited to any but a most primitive economy. It is true that the evolution of *jhuming* method marked an important change in the history of development of agriculture. But the practice has long become outdated and is in any case not compatible with economic change and development".

The socio-economic resurvey of Khejurbond, a Dimasa village in North Cachar Hills reveals, "Average *jhum* land per household in 1983 is found to be 0.68 hectare as against 1.46 hectares in 1977. The realisation of the wasteful use of *jhum* land and uneconomic production are responsible for decline in area under *jhum* cultivation" (Borah, 1985 : 47).

In a study on the problems of agricultural development in the Hill Areas of Assam, Goswami and Saha (1969 : 20) have mentioned, "*Jhuming,* a shifting form of cultivation is predominant against settled farming. This form of cultivation is wrongly thought to be a way of life. In actual fact, *jhuming* is the only feasible way of raising food from rugged hill slopes. But where the tribal people have found alternative better system of farming, they have accepted the alternative. It is well known that the Apatanis cultivate wet paddy in irrigated field, the Angami Nagas grow rice from terraced field even in steep slopes. 75% of the Khasis and about 40% of the Garos have already given up *jhuming* in favour of settled farming. As a matter of policy, we shall have to create conditions favourable for gradual change from hunting and gathering to settled agriculture. As such, it shall not be looked down upon, rather, where shifting cultivation will be the only system of using hill slopes, it should be made scientific. *Jhum* cultivation should not be allowed in steep slopes and catchment areas of the hills. In the abandoned *jhum* fields, afforestation shall have to be made with the initiative of the Forest Department so that the soil erosion and flood (in the plains below) is minimised".

The socio-economic survey of Mawtnum (1963-64), a Khasi village of Meghalaya, reveals, "The influence of *jhuming* is gradually declining because of its low return of output per acre and per man hour and this has been amply indicated by the small number of households (only 17.14% of the total) pursuing *jhum* cultivation in the village. Another reason for weaning away influence of *jhuming* may also be well-attributed to the fact that the village has assumed more or less the character of a settled village with no further intention of shifting elsewhere in future. With it the economic implication of settled farming in the area appears to have been more enhanced than before" (Gohain, 1969 : 157).

While dealing with the socio-economic study at Banshidua, a Garo village of Meghalaya, Saha & Barkataky (1969 : 230) opine, "In a pre-industrial society under the conditions of limited resources, as population increases, agriculture also changes from extensive land use as in case of *jhuming* to intensive land use as in settled farming. The process affects the entire agricultural structure, in particular the land tenure system, pattern of cropping, and tools and implements. But in respect of input-output relationship, the change becomes most spectacular. In *jhuming,* there is very little inputs except human labour and home produced seed (which also embodies only human labour), but in settled agriculture the inputs are many and varied. The output is very much dependent on other inputs except labour. The labour's input-output relationships in jhuming and settled farming may weigh with the shifting cultivators in case of change to the latter system. While rising population pressure and deteriorating productivity of *jhuming* are compelling the people to fall upon settled farming, the fall in return to labour (marginal productivity labour, we may say) will act as a disincentive to adoption of settled farming. Thus, if the *jhumias* are left to their fate and the process is allowed to operate automatically, the distress of the people will be quite great. Undernutrition, disease, famine and consequent loss of life will be the results. Viewing the prospect from both economic and humanitarian standpoints, the process should not be allowed to go unheeded. This underlies the importance of planned change over from *jhuming* to settled farming".

The North Eastern Council, Shillong has initiated "interactions with the State Governments of the North Eastern Region as also other Central Organisations operating in the region on the problems of shifting cultivation and sponsored a number of schemes putting emphasis on the varied aspects of the intricacies of the *jhuming.* The NEC sponsored schemes have highlighted among other things (a) protection of the forests for maintaining the ecological balance in the region (b) permanent settlement of the jhumias as a solid solution (c) sufficient support to the cultivators in the form of subsidised fertilizers, pesticides, seeds and traction power (d) improvement of communication links" (*Hazarika*, 1988 : 18).

While referring to alternative land use systems for replacement of *jhuming,* Prasad, Singh & Varma (1990 : 143) note, "The system (shifting cultivation) in the present context has become not only unproductive but also hazardous to the environment. Exposure of rocks due to soil erosion, heavy silt load in stream and drying of perennial water resources, loss of plant nutrients, loss of forestry resources, loss of flora of human and animal importance, are some of the major hazardous effects of the shifting cultivation. ICAR Research Complex for NEH Region is working on various alternative farming systems to shifting cultivation on watershed basis. Alternative land uses are agriculture, horticulture, livestock, forestry, fishery and combination of these. These are being supported by mechanical conservation measures like contour bunding, bench terracing, contour trenching, half-moon terracing, small check dams and grassed waterways etc. Out of the various land use combinations under trials the best and ideal system suited to hill slopes is, it seems to be, agri-horti-silvipastoral system. The system comprises agricultural land use towards the foothills, horticulture in the mid portion of the hill and silvipastoral land use towards the top of the hill. Land development may cost about 190 man days/ha. Such land uses are expected to retain over 90 per cent of annual rainfall in situ with negligible soil losses from the system."

Various experiments have also been carried out by the Agricultural Research Station, Diphu to provide alternative to shifting cultivation. In this respect Sarma et al (1996) opine," Efforts are being made to find out improved practices identical to jhuming, but more productive and less injurious to soil and environments. Improved technologies in the place of shifting cultivation in the *jhum* land have already been identified and recommended for general cultivation. The technologies include (1) replacement of traditional varieties by the improved ones, (2) use of manures and fertilizers to maintain soil fertility, (3) inclusion of perennial horticultural crops along with agronomic crops to encourage settled cultivation, (4) judicious crop selection and placing them in scientific manner for better production and utilization of land. It was reported that growing pineapple, turmeric, ginger and arum in the border; and rice, maize, sesame and cotton in line across the slope in the middle, significantly out-yielded traditional *jhum* in terms of rice-equivalent yield (Sarma et al. 1995: 196-201)."

Under the technical guidance of Roy Burman, an Ao Naga village named Warmung was investigated by Ao in the year 1966. In this context Roy Burman (1970 : 325) observes, "Shifting cultivation by slash and burn method is by far the most important type of agriculture followed in the village. The following reasons were given by the villagers for their attachment to shifting cultivation: (1) Nature of the terrain is unfit for wet or terrace cultivation (2) Plots for wet cultivation are small and scattered (3) Fear of wild animals to reach the scattered plots fit for wet cultivation (4) Difficulty in making roads to reach the scattered plots fit for wet cultivation at long distances (5) Rivers are deep and it is difficult to construct irrigation channels (6) Lack of finance for irrigation."

With regard to the prevalence of shifting cultivation in Arunachal Pradesh, Dutta (1989 : 42) comments, "Although alternative measures to *jhum* cultivation have been in the offing the prospect of complete abolition of shifting cultivation is very bleak mainly due to the nature of the topography coupled with the traditional attachment of the people to the age-old system. In fact, the entire socio-cultural life of the people is very intimately connected with *jhuming* since time immemorial."

Referring to *jhum* among the Wanchos of Tirap district of Arunachal Pradesh, Sachchidananda (1988 : 61) concludes, "Shifting cultivation cannot be viewed as an economic activity since all economic relations are set in a social framework. The entire social life of the community may revolve round the practice of swiddening. But each case of swiddening has to be studied in its specific historical, physiographic and socio-political contexts. Among the Wanchos it is closely integrated with their political and social systems. The Chief holds absolute power over land commonly owned and distributes land to heads of households according to their needs as well as their capacity to cultivate the land. Since no private ownership of land is acknowledged, there is no incentive among the people to the development of their land as they would like to enhance their own income. Endemic wars and rains in the past increased the powers of the chief. If people had to supplement their income, it was only their working as casual daily labourers in road connection work or in various plantations. In some cases even in the Wancho area, people are aware of the soil erosion and they have devised mechanisms to reduce it to the minimum. Lastly, there is the question of availability of plains land upon which people can be resettled. In view of these factors it has not been possible to reduce the coverage of swiddening in the Wancho areas. But it is not the faith in traditional practices and rituals that are responsible for this."

Besides, Ganguly (1969) conducted a study on the economics problems of the *jhumias* of Tripura. Saha (1970) made a detailed study on the economics of shifting cultivation in Assam.

Kaith (1956)* carried out a study on the extent of shifting cultivation practised by various tribes of India with emphasis on the number of tribal households involved with it, total area of land utilized and various crops cultivated. Roy Burman and Sharma (1970) made a study on the shifting cultivation practised by the different tribes of the country. Bose (1967) provided a comparative study in respect of carrying capacity of land under shifting cultivation in South Mizoram, Keonjhar Hills and Abujhmer Hills. Nag (1958) highlights the economic system of the Baigas of Madhya Pradesh. Mahapatra and Kiranbala (1972-73) and Patnaik (1977) dealt with shifting cultivation prevalent in Orissa. Vidyarthi (1963)* highlighted nature-man-spirit complex among the Malers of Bihar.

The practice of shifting cultivation has been a controversial matter among the scholars. Some are in favour of it while others are against this practice. Chaturvedi, the former Inspector General of Forests to the Government of India carried out an investigation into the forestry problems in Assam in the year 1953 and remarked that shifting cultivation could not be held responsible for soil erosion. Elwin (1964 : 81) opines, "It is sometimes said that the floods which from time to time devastate the plains of Assam are due to the practice of *jhuming* in the NEFA (Arunachal Pradesh) hills. But this cannot be so, for the conditions of rainfall, humidity and temperature in the *jhum* areas of NEFA are so favourable that no clearing remains without a vegetal cover for any length of time. Immediately after any area goes fallow at the close of the cropping period, it is covered

* Cited in Sachchidananda (1989 :5).

with some kind of vegetation which checks erosion and the run-off of rain-water. Moreover, the area under cropping at any one time is estimated at only 3 to 4 per cent of the total area of the Agency. It is the loss of soil fertility rather than the danger of erosion and leaching, which is the real problem". Shivaraman, the Adviser to the Programme Administration of the Planning Commission in 1957 opined, "It is a mistake to assume that shifting cultivation in itself is unscientific land use. Actually, it is practical approach to certain inherent difficulties in preparing a proper seed bed in steep slopes where any disturbance of the surface by hoeing or ploughing will result in washing away of the fertile top soil. The tribal people, therefore, take care not to plough or disturb the soil before sowing. The destruction of weeds and improvement of tilth necessary for a proper seed-bed are achieved with the help of fire. In most of the interior areas, where communication is not developed and not sufficient land suitable for terracing is available *jhuming* alone can be done for the present and as such every effort should be made to improve the fertility of the *jhum land"* (*Bhowmick,* 1990 : 106).

On the other hand, various allegations against this method of cultivation have also been reported. While giving evidence before the Partially Excluded Areas Enquiry Committee of Orissa Mr. Nicholson, the Conservator of Forests maintained, "The damage done to the forests by shifting cultivation is serious and that only under certain conditions where the area of land available is large and population small, such cultivation does little harm". Dr. N.L.Bor, Forest Botanist in the Forest Research Institute at Dehradun in his presidential address to the Section of Botany of the Indian Science Congress in 1942 observes, "Of all practices initiated by man, the most noxius is that of Shifting Cultivation". He attributes the cause of soil erosion in the Assam Hills to the practice of shifting cultivation. Another writer in reviewing the *Report of Forest Administration in Assam for 1940-41 in Nature* 1942 calls shifting cultivation, "the most wasteful of agricultural methods" (Gohain, 1994: 188).

In tune with these observations, Majumdar (1990 : 31), from an anthropological intensive investigation maintains, "We should not deny the fact that shifting cultivation is becoming more and more destructive of ecological balance and we should not argue for its continuance by saying that it is a way of life and that destroying the way of life will mean destroying the people themselves. The shifting cultivators have themselves understood that their method of cultivation is fighting a losing battle and that is why, they themselves are trying to adopt other methods or whenever opportunity offers change over to other occupation."

Under the circumstances, it has been imperative on the part of the Government and other concerned agencies to take appropriate measures to regulate and control this practice for a long- term welfare of the *Jhumias*, inhabiting the different parts of the country. An overall idea about the different schemes taken up in this direction in the Karbi Anglong district in Assam has been provided in the next chapter. The problem at hand for the present study has also been spelt out in *Chapter Two*.

II

THE PROBLEM

In order to regulate and control the practice of shifting cultivation in the district of Karbi Anglong various measures have been adopted by the concerned authorities. In accordance with the provisions of the Sixth Schedule to the Constitution of India, the Mikir Hills District *(Jhuming)* Regulation was passed by the District Council in 1954. According to this Regulation, the boundaries of each village would be fixed by the District Council. The shifting of the villages from the existing sites without the previous permission of the Executive Committee of the District Council is prohibited. Nobody is allowed to practise *jhuming* or cut trees within a radius of half a mile from the boundary of the village. The Executive Committee will also fix the rotation period of *jhuming* on certain portions of the village and the area to be *jhumed* by an individual cultivator. Any person who contravenes the provisions of the Regulation will be liable to a fine extending upto Rs. 500.00. In this context, it may be pointed out here that the rights of selecting *jhum* plots and distributing them among the families as per their requirement by the traditional village councils have been curtailed by this Regulation. Bordoloi (1990 : 34) in this context reports, "Since the provisions of this Regulation had centralised all powers relating to the regulation of the *Jhuming* to the Executive Committee of the District Council, the people had a great resentment. To decentralise the matters the Mikir Hills District *(Jhuming)* Regulation of 1954 was amended in 1966."

According to the Mikir Hills District *(Jhuming) (Amended)* Regulation, 1966, *jhuming* "shall be gregarious and restricted to one particular area for a village irrespective of the number of families *jhuming* and shall be selected by the villagers in consultation with *Sarkari*

Gaonburas and the local *Mouzadar* in accordance with the provisions of this Regulation. In case of any disagreement about selection of *jhuming* site among the villagers, *Sarkari Gaonburas* and *Mouzadars* shall refer it to the Executive Committee and the decision of the Executive Committee in this respect shall be final. Individual plots within the selected area may be selected by the people themselves in consultation with the local *Sarkari Gaonbura.* The villagers shall be jointly responsible for any damage to the areas not selected for *jhuming* by spreading of fire from *jhumed* areas. *Jhuming* within two gunter's chain of any perennial stream on either or within one gunter's chain of any State Public Works Department and District Council roads respectively is prohibited. Any area which is covered by *Sal* or other valuable trees shall not be selected or allotted for *jhum.* The District Council reserves the right to dispose of the felled stuff in *jhum* areas in any manner it considers suitable without interfering *jhuming*" (District Council Code, 1987 : 38).

During the different Five Year Plan periods the Development Departments viz., Agriculture, Irrigation, Soil Conservation, P.W.D., Sericulture, Forest and Assam Plantation Crops Development Corporation etc., have adopted certain measures to do away with shifting cultivation in the Karbi Anglong district. In this context mention may be made of the schemes for establishment of model villages, cash crop plantation and composite projects etc. The scheme for establishment of model villages was implemented in 1960s in ten villages of the district with financial assistance from the District Council and the Government of Assam. The villages are (1) Hongkram (2) Tarabasa (3) Samelangso (4) Uttar Barbil (5) Chilimkhowa (6) Rongjangphong (7) Chokihola (8) Bhoni (9) Chutianala and (10) Bomroi. While dealing with the model villages, Bordoloi (1990 : 240) comments, "As a first step for the rehabilitation of the *jhumias* the Mikir Hills District Council had established model villages (*Adarsha Gaon*) in different areas of the district wherein Karbi *jhumias* were brought down from the hill tops and settled in the plains portion of the district. The scheme is partially successful. The reasons for partial failure of the scheme, according to my opinion, are the following: Firstly, there has been no follow-up programme at all. After the establishment of a full-fledged model village providing all the basic amenities nothing has so far been done to induce the people to stay there. As a consequence, many Karbi families have already left the model villages and gone to their old hill top habitats. Secondly, since the construction of the houses no repairing has been done by the people inspite of abundance of building materials near their abodes. In fact, the size of the typed house is too big for a family to manage. Thirdly, it is found that many families instead of living in the houses given by the District Council, are putting up in houses constructed by themselves in the backyards in their traditional pattern. The typed houses constructed by the District Council are not only too big but are quite different also from the traditional pattern. The people would not have abandoned these houses had they been constructed in traditional pattern with improvement. Thus in rehabilitating the *jhumias* in the model villages, these sociological factors have not at all been taken into consideration."

Cash crop plantation scheme involves the plantation of coffee, rubber, black pepper and cashewnut etc. Initially, the Soil Conservation Department, Government of Assam implemented the scheme. Later on, with the creation of the Assam Plantation Crops Development Corporation (APCDC) on 1st September, 1974, the scheme was handed over to the Corporation by the Department of Soil Conservation. The coffee and rubber plantations under the APCDC have shown encouraging results. In the Karbi Anglong district there are a total of 5 (five) coffee estates with a total area of 531.95 hectares and 10 (ten) rubber estates with a total area of 1006.25 hectares. Moreover, the Diphu Central Rubber Nursery has an area of 3.00 hectares. In fact, the plantations after maturity have to be handed over to the *jhumia* beneficiaries @ one hectare per family. But complete transfer has not yet taken place due to some reasons although the main objectives of the Corporation are to rehabilitate the *jhumias* and to accelerate the pace of economic development among the tribal people living in the hills.

With the intention of checking depletion of forest cover and inducing the *jhumias* for settled cultivation, the Planning Commission introduced the interdisciplinary programme 'Composite Project' from 1974-75 with financial involvement of Rs.12.15 crore under Special Central Assistance in the two hill districts of Assam. Some of the villages brought under the Composite Project are Sikari Bey (Karbi), Borlangfer (Karbi), Harseali-Siloni (Karbi), Chutianala (Karbi), Kheroni (Karbi and Dimasa Kachari), Rongagora (Karbi), Gudan Ingti (Karbi), Chowkihola (Karbi) and Bura Tisso (Karbi) in Karbi Anglong and Retzol (Hmar), Jatinga-Lampo (Dimasa Kachari), Pura (Dimasa Kachari) Natun Leikul (Kuki), Daudung (Dimasa Kachari) and Baojan (Dimasa Kachari) in North Cachar Hills. The amount mentioned above was allocated to (1) Reclamation and Terracing (2) Minor Irrigation (3) Plantation (4) Agricultural Inputs and Extension (5) Afforestation and (6) Infrastructure and growth points. Altogether an amount of Rs.16.50 crore was utilised for this project from 1974-75 to 1981-82. "The Cash Crop Plantation Programme formed the nucleus of the Composite Project. The other five components provided the subsidiary base for the resettlement programme. The activities of the interrelated sectors were sought to be brought under the common umbrella of supervision and implementation. Emphasis was given to Coffee and Rubber plantation on *Jhum* lands by engaging *jhumia* families. After maturity...these plantations were expected to be handed over to the *jhumia* families. For this purpose, Assam Plantation Crops Development Corporation (APCDC) was formed in the latter part of 1974. The objectives envisaged under the 'Composite Project' could not be fully achieved primarily due to lack of effective integration of the intersectoral schemes. The schemes were executed more or less on departmental lines somewhat to the detriment of the common goal for resettlement of the *jhumias*. The other drawbacks were (1) Non-conferment of land rights to *jhumia* families over developed lands (2) Non-involvement of beneficiary families at different stages of the Project (3) Non-evolution of a sound strategy based on local conditions, endowments and felt needs and (4) starting of large scale schemes without first trying them on pilot scheme basis" (*Draft Eight Five Year Plan,* 1992-97).

The Planning Commission reviewed the performance of the Composite Project in December, 1981 and decided to replace it by the *Integrated Jhumia Development Programme* (IJDP). In the districts of Karbi Anglong and North Cachar Hills the IJDP has been implemented out of the fund available through Special Central Assistance under the State Plan. It is an entrusted scheme of the respective District Councils.

"For achieving tangible results in inducing a tribal family to change over from *jhum* life-style to any settled mode of living, one has to keep in mind these three aspects- (a) besides promotion of ecology it should be acceptable to a tribal (b) stable foodstuff of the people is to be provided at reasonable price at the doorstep (c) provision of avenues for amusement and recreations to fit into tribal ethos. On the basis of these recommendations, the scheme of *Integrated Jhumia Development Programme* has been suitably modified to meet the needs adequately" (*Hasao Bubli*, 1988).

Under this programme, provision of reclaimed land/terraced land with irrigation facilities, construction of worksheds for weaving, knitting, tailoring & carpentry etc., and establishment of nursery for selling seedlings are some of the common economic benefits to be derived by the people. Among individual family oriented benefits mention may be made of supply of equipments for weaving and sericulture etc., poultry, piggery, duckery, fishery and horticulture according to the felt needs of the tribal families. Moreover, infrastructural facilities like construction of vehicular road, provision of drinking water viz., installation of tubewell/ringwell, health services, primary education etc., are also taken into consideration. Large Area Multipurpose Co-operative Societies (LAMPS) have to open retail outlets in the vicinity of the concerned villages so that the people do not face any difficulty in procuring rice and other essential commodities. Emphasis has also been given to provide grants-in-aid to the local Youth Clubs from the Government for recreation and amusement.

Eleven experimental centres under *Integrated Jhumia Development Programme*–6 (six) in Karbi Anglong and 5 (five) in North Cachar Hills were taken up since the last part of 1982-83. These are Karbi Rongsopi (Karbi), Kumpahar (Karbi), Hongkloyadong (Karbi), Kheroni (Dimasa Kachari), Bura Tisso (Karbi) and Sinanadi (Karbi) in Karbi Anglong and Amrudisa (Dimasa Kachari), Digendu Part IV (Dimasa Kachari), Boromoulkoi (Hmar), Indrimbunglow (Jeme Naga) and Natun Leikul (Kuki) in North Cachar Hills. However, implementation of the schemes at Sinanadi has been discontinued since 1983-84. The financial and physical achievements in respect of ten centres for the period from 1982-83 to 1986-87 in the two hill districts are furnished in Table II.1. The table shows that as a result of implementation of various schemes involving an expenditure of Rs.72.08 lakh during the period of five years, the number of families completely weaned away from *jhum* is 214 (53.37%) out of the total number of 401 families. Again, the net area under *jhum* and the total area released from *jhum* in case of ten centres are furnished in Table II.2. The table reveals that out of 675.11 hectares of net area under *jhum*, the area of land released from *jhum* is 583.21 hectares in the centres.

Bordoloi (1990 : 40) mentions, "A research study carried out in 1983 by Dr. D.N. Majumdar of Anthropology Department of Gauhati University on 'Evaluation and Monitoring of the Integrated *Jhumia* Development Projects in Hill Areas of Assam' shows that the villagers are not involved at the planning stage. The common villagers except two or three village leaders are not aware of the details of the scheme, the kind of inputs they are going to receive, the type of work they are expected to do and money they would get for making available their services. Dr. Majumdar has also pointed out that the sites for location of these projects were not properly selected and the resource potentials were taken into account only after the selection of sites. This study further reveals that even in the selection of beneficiaries proper care has not been taken. Some of the real *jhumia* families inhabiting the vicinity of the projects have been denied of the benefits. It is a fact that the *Integrated Jhumia Development Projects* are working better than those of the erstwhile Composite Projects. These projects were initiated only in 1982-83. Basing on the *jhumia* families, the Government is going to have some more such projects in the two Hill Districts of Assam in near future. Since no field evaluation has so far been done on these projects by any outside agency, it is very difficult to say at this stage the actual benefits people have been deriving from these projects and how far the incidence of *jhum* cultivation has gone down because of the functioning of these projects".

In order to gain an insight into the workings of the pilot projects (experimental centres) under the IJDP, a detailed note of evaluation of Boromoulkoi IJDP (prepared by the Divisional Officer, Haflong Soil Conservation Division & Project Officer, IJDP, Boromoulkoi) received from the Secretary (T), Executive Committee, N.C.Hills Autonomous District Council, Haflong has been reproduced below:

"The Boromoulkoi IJDP was initially started in the year 1982-83, where some Soil Conservation works like terracing was taken up. The progress of the work was not very satisfactory as the beneficiaries to whom the works were entrusted, could not even complete 10% of the work. During 1983-84, a land reclamation scheme was taken up and the target was achieved in full swing during the year.

Before launching of the IJDP activities in the Boromoulkoi Project 45 families were practising *jhum* cultivation for their livelihood to the tune of 315 *bighas**. But after taking up of different schemes, a gradual trend of reduction of *jhuming* practices was noticed year after year. In the initial stage each *jhumia* family took up 7 *bighas* of land on average for *jhuming*

* 1 bigha = 0.13387 hectares or 0.33058 acres.

* 1 : 4 means 1 male and 4 females.

and now a stage has reached that only five families are in the habit of practising *jhum* cultivation to the extent of 30 *bighas* till 31.12.86. Out of 45 families, 40 numbers have almost abandoned *jhuming* practices and they are adhering to wet paddy cultivation and other agricultural crops within and around the Project Area. Five families who are still in the habit of practising *jhum* have got sufficient number of grown up children and some of them are engaged in *jhum* cultivation for getting extra remuneration. But an urge has developed among the villagers for changing over to permanent agriculture and thereby all the *jhumia* families will be completely weaned away from *jhuming* within a very short period.

Almost all the inputs supplied by various departments are being used at their individual level. Departments like Agriculture, Veterinary, Industry, Fishery, Handloom and Weaving are involved in supply of various inputs, livestock, machineries etc., to the beneficiaries. One fishery has been developed by the Department of Fisheries on individual level.The Department of Agriculture has provided with 4 (four) sugarcane crushers at group level. The main link road developed by the Soil Conservation and one community hall constructed within the village from M.R.E.P. scheme are being utilised at community level.

During 1984-85, 45 families have developed 256 *bighas* of land in course of implementing horticulture crops: Ginger–141 *bighas*, Banana–38 *bighas,* Orange –17 *bighas,* Pineapple –18 *bighas,* Arecanut – 37 bighas and Sugarcane – 5 bighas. Further, Animal Husbandry & Veterinary Department has supplied the following livestock according to the needs of the beneficiaries: Bullock–21 pair, Pultry (1 : 4)–13 units*, Piggery (1 : 2)– 4 units, K.C.Duck (1 : 4)–12 units and Feeding through –13 nos.

During 1985-86, 45 (forty five) families have developed 161 bighas of land for raising the following crops: Orange–33 *bighas,* Ginger–237 *bighas*, Pineapple–19 *bighas*, Banana–37 *bighas,* Arecanut–36 *bighas* and Sugarcane–6 *bighas.* The distribution of livestock from A.H. & Vety., during 1985-86 is not yet fully met. The reason of shortfall is not known. However, the matter is being pursued with the concerned department.

During 1986-87, 45 (forty five) families have developed 161 *bighas* of land till 31.12.86 and raised different horticulture crops therein as in 1985-86. In addition, the Department of Industries has supplied the following articles according to the needs of the people : Hand sewing machine-10 nos., Carpentry set–10 nos. and Blacksmithy–5 nos.

TABLE II.1

Financial and physical achievement relating to ten experimental centres during 1982-87

District	*Financial allocation received (lakhs)*	*Expenditure (lakhs)*	*Land development/ Terraced*		*Number of jhumia families*		*Number of jhumia families completely weaned away*
			Target (ha)	*Achievement (ha)*	*Target (No.)*	*Covered (No.)*	
1	*2*	*3*	*4*	*5*	*6*	*7*	*8*
Karbi Anglong	47.84	33.50	311	420.55	194	203	171
N.C. Hills		53.41	38.58	286	152.46	215	198 43
Total	101.25	72.08	597	573.01	409	401	214

Source : *Draft Eighth Five Year Plan, 1992-97*. Development Commissioner for the Hill Areas, Assam.

TABLE II.2

Net area under jhum and total area released from jhum in case of ten experimental centres

District	*Total area (ha)*	*Net area under jhum as per annual Progress Report (ha)*	*Area released from jhum (ha)*
1	*2*	*3*	*4*
Karbi Anglong	586	469.21	420.55
N.C. Hills	9843	205.90	162.66
Total	10429	675.11	583.21

Source : *Draft Eighth Five Year Plan, 1992-97.* Development Commissioner for the Hill Areas, Assam.

As already pointed out, 315 *bighas* of land were under *jhuming* before launching of IJDP schemes. In 1983-84, 225 *bighas* of land were under *jhum* cultivation and in 1984-85, it has been reduced to 144 *bighas* while in 1985-86, it has again gone down to 72 *bighas* and at the end of 1986 it stands at 30 *bighas* only.

Very often complaints have been received from the beneficiaries regarding the delay in receiving inputs particularly from Agriculture Department. This is, of course, an important aspect and the matter is conveyed to the concerned department for timely supply of agriculture inputs and seeds so that the time schedule for a particular crop is fruitfully utilised. Further, it is often said that some crops are infested with different kinds of diseases and as such, application of insecticides is needed in time. The department concerned is apprised of taking timely action to tide over the difficulties. Plant pathologists in this direction need to visit the Project at frequent interval and suggest remedial measures to be taken at the site accordingly. The same problem is also noticed in respect of livestock supplied by the Veterinary Department. Some improved variety of poultry supplied to the villagers died of diseases and the local variety of poultry got infested and thereby large scale mortalities took place. Due to communication gap, timely action could not be taken to get rid of the diseases. So remedial measures are to be found out in this direction by the concerned department so that the villagers are not deprived of getting free and timely service in such matter in future. It may be relevantly noted here that the villagers are very much inclined to switch over to wet cultivation on the valley bottom land along Jatinga river and about 20 *jhumia* families are doing wet cultivation. There is scope of doing double and multiple cropping in the land so available, provided irrigation facilities, supply of improved variety of seeds and fertilisers can be made available to them. The gross income after implementation of IJDP schemes till August, 1986 stands as Rs.3,11,747,00.

In case of release of fund some difficulities are experienced. Timely release of fund is very essential. The matter needs a further review for taking necessary corrective measures".

An evaluation study conducted by Sharmathakur (1990 : 245) in Kheroni village which was brought under the Integrated *Jhumia* Development Programme in 1982-83 reveals, "The village Kheroni lying at a distance of about 13 km. from Diphu is inhabited by the Dimasa

Kacharis consisting of about 150 households. Under the Integrated *Jhumia* Development Programme 30 hectares of land have been distributed among 28 families for orange, pineapple and coconut cultivation. The indicidual beneficiary scheme was also implemented and pig, goat, poultry, plough-cattle were distributed among the villagers. Besides, weaving and blacksmithy schemes were also implemented. Under the Integrated Rural Development Programme (IRDP) loan-cum-subsidy worth of Rupees Two Thousand was sanctioned to each selected villager for purchase of bullocks. It was reported that middlemen or agents play their roles while processing loan proposals and in most cases the beneficiaries have been deprived of the real benefits.........Shri Mani Chandra Bey of Kheroni Gaon lamented that he got Rs.1300.00 only although the authorities had sanctioned Rs. 2000.00 for him for a pair of bullocks".

The observation makes it apparent that notwithstanding some operational flaws, all possible efforts are being made by the Government to wean the *jhumias* away from the shifting cultivation. Achievement in respect of all the ten IJDP centres (experimental) during the period 1982-83 to 1985-86 has been furnished in Table II.3. The table reveals that the development departments viz., Soil Conservation, Agriculture, Animal Husbandry and Fisheries etc., have implemented various schemes not only to ameliorate the poor economic condition of the people inhabiting the centres but also to attract the people towards settled mode of livelihood without practising the harmful method of shifting cultivation.

Taking into consideration the encouraging results obtained from the ten IJDP experimental centres the Government has taken a decision to implement welfare schemes under the IJDP in 40 (forty) centres of Karbi Anglong and North Cachar Hills, covering 20 (twenty) centres in each district for a period of five years from 1986-87. However, six centres – three in each district were abandoned due to some reasons and as a result, 34 (thirty four) centres covering 2157 households (1055 in Karbi Anglong and 1102 in North Cachar Hills) were continued upto 1990-91. Rs. 572.00 lakhs were allotted against these centres for a period of five years from 1986-87 to 1990-91. In this context, it may be noted here that since the physical and financial targets during 1986-87 could not be achieved due to some unavoidable circumstances, works in respect of 34 (thirty four) centres were continued upto March, 1992 and the amount of expenditure was to the tune of Rs.408.93 lakhs. This programme mainly involved two components (1) Beneficiary Oriented Schemes and (2) Loan Scheme provided to the Assam Plantation Crops Development Corporation (APCDC) for cash crop plantations viz., coffee and rubber which should be transferred to the *jhumia* beneficiaries after maturity. The names of the centres alongwith total households at the time of implementation of the schemes are furnished in Table II.4 for Karbi Anglong and North Cachar Hills.

In the year 1986 a Watershed Management Project was also launched at Hirhiri Barpanjan located within the jurisdictions of Nilip Development Block, Chokihola in the district of Karbi Anglong. The project with a coverage of 2300 hectares of land aims at providing benefits to the total population of about 2020 belonging to 324 Karbi and Thengal Kachari households in 23 villages. Most of the households carry out both *jhum* and settled cultivation for their livelihood. However, 25 (twenty five) households practise *jhum* exclusively. Financial assistance for carrying out the project was available from the North Eastern Council, Shillong as well as the State Government. The Department of Agriculture was the nodal agency for the project. The names of the villages under the project have been furnished in Table II.5.

As per the instruction of the Ministry of Agriculture, Government of India two Compact Areas were selected in the Hill Areas of Assam under Central Sector *Jhum* Control Programme. The programme was launched in September, 1989. In the Karbi Anglong district the project area is located within Chinthong Development Block of the Hamren subdivision while in the North Cachar Hills district the project area Hadingma is located within Jatinga Valley Development Block and Diyung Valley Development Block. The former covers 1488 households of 36 villages while the latter covers 1076 households of 40 villages. The Ministry of Agriculture, Government of India released an amount of Rs.324.50 lakhs under the scheme for control of shifting cultivation with central assistance for the period from 1988-89 to 1990-91. The villages taken up under Chinthong Compact Area Development Programme (CADP) are shown in Table II.6 while those of Hadingma CADP are shown in Table II.7.

A status paper on the Central Sector *Jhum* Control Programme prepared by the Development Commissioner for Hill Areas, Assam (1991 : 16) reveals, "A major factor in the successful implementation of the programme was the unstinted co-operation from the beneficiaries. Village Developmental Committees were constituted for informal consultations as well as overseeing the implementation of the development programmes at the village level. The residents of the project area have shown great interest in the scheme and its implementation and offered constructive suggestions in the matter of drawing up and finalising of village level plans. As the funds available under the Central Sector programme are limited and the expenditure levels under various items had been pre-determined, the project authority had to seek the assistance of other developmental departments for pooling their resource under the Sectoral plans. It is gratifying to note that the response from other departments was spontaneous and this has contributed to successful launching of the programme. The departments have in general helped in maintaining the work schedules as originally planned. A major hurdle faced during the implementation was some delay in the release of requisite fund. Obviously untimely release of fund hampered continuous implementation and often valuable working time was lost due to the same. The limited span of working season, difficult terrain, lack of all weather approach roads, absence of adequate infrastructural facilities etc., were other bottlenecks in the implemention".

An evaluation study was conducted by the District Research Office, Diphu in the year 1992 in eight CADP villages–five from Karbi Anglong and three from North Cachar Hills on the basis of random sampling. The Karbi Anglong villages are Borpu, Umpanchi, Harlongjuwe, Socheng and Umcherra while the N.C.Hills villages are Guliabra, Lungkhok and Thaisilinghawar. The selected villages consist of 300 households with a total population of 1633, the males and females being 874 (53.52%) and 759 (46.48%) respectively. The study reports,... In order to wean away the *jhumias* from the age-old method of shifting cultivation, various types of schemes have been implemented in the surveyed villages. Some of the schemes are (i) Land Development (ii) Animal Husbandry (iii) Pisciculture (iv) Water Harvest Structure (v) Cottage Industry (vi) Handloom and Textiles (vii) Plantation Crops/Horticultural Crops/Orchards and (vii) Agricultural Inputs etc.

(i) One of the important schemes under this programme is land development which included reclaimed or terraced land for the purpose of wet and *rabi* cultivation. The total area of terraced/reclaimed land in the surveyed villages is 111.43 hectares. (ii) with regard to veterinary inputs it may be said that buffaloes, milch cows, goats, ducks, pigs and poultry

TABLE II.3

Achievement on IJDP for the period 1982-83 to 1985-86

Sl. No.	Name of the IJDP	1982-83 Target	1982-83 Achievement	1983-84 Target	1983-84 Achievement	1984-85 Target	1984-85 Achievement	1985-86 Target	1985-86 Achievement
1	*2*	*3*	*4*	*5*	*6*	*7*	*8*	*9*	*10*
	KARBI ANGLONG DISTRICT								
1	KHERONI								
		Jungle clearing, ploughing and harrowing=30 ha	22.00 ha	Jungle clearing, ploughing and harrowing=30 ha	30.00 ha	Levelling and tractorisation= 50.00 ha	50.00 ha	Seeds = 15q	14.49 q
								Seedling Grafts = 0.35 lakhs	0.35 lakhs
		Seeds = 4.50 q	4.50 q	Seeds = 10 q	9.50 q	Seeds =10.85 q	10.85 q	Horticultural garden=10 nos.	10 nos.
		Seedlings/Grafts = 0.11 lakhs	0.11 lakhs	Ginger rhizome = 7.80 q	7.80 q	Seedlings/Grafts =0.005 lakhs	0.005 lakhs	Poultry = 10 units	10 units
		Pesticides= 16.50 q	16.50 q	Seedlings/Grafts = 0.004 lakhs	0.004 lakhs			Loom = 10 units	10 units
		Fireextinguisher= –	46 nos.					Blacksmithy– 5 units	5 units
								Ringwell -1 no.	1 no

2 KUMPAHAR					
Reclamation 30ha	28.20 ha	Reclamation– 24 ha	24.00 ha	Bench terracing 5.00 ha	4.97 ha
Prutерican terracing-25 ha	24.50 ha	Bench terracing 9 ha	8.27 ha	Prutерican terracing–10 ha	10.00 ha
Valley bottom land development 22 ha	21.56 ha	Water distribution– 15 ha	15.0 ha	Water distribution– 40 ha	40.00 ha

continued ....

TABLE II.3

Achievement on IJDP for the period 1982-83 to 1985-86

1	*2*	*3*	*4*	*5*	*6*	*7*	*8*	*9*	*10*
2 KUMPAHAR									
	Camp hut-1 no.		1 no.	Afforestation 56 ha	56.00 ha	Afforestation– 56 ha	56.00 ha		
				Nursery - 0.25 ha	0.25 ha				
				Approach Road 400 R.M.	400 R.M.				
3 KARBI RONGSOPI									
	Reclamation 40 ha		40.00 ha	Reclamation 70 ha	70.00 ha	Reclamation– 50 ha	50.00 ha		
				Ringwell–2 nos.	2 nos.				
				Camp hut–1no.	1no.				
4 BURA TISSO									
	Reclamation/ ploughing & harrowing– 5 ha		5.00 ha	Reclamation & tractorisation– 8 ha	8.00 ha	Seeds– 15.25 q	15.25 q	Reclamation & tractorisation– 16 ha	15.07 ha

Continued........

	Irrigation– 5 ha	5.00 ha	Seeds– 4.18 q	4.18 q			Seeds – 26 q	26.00 q
	Seeds– 26q	26q	Small agricultural implements– 40 units	40 units				
5 HONKGLOYADONG	Reclamation– 26 ha	26.00 ha	Ploughing & harrowing– 26 ha	26.00 ha	Tractorisation– 80 ha	78.42 ha		
	Seedlings/ Grafts– 0.05 lakhs	0.05 lakhs	Water distribution 26 ha	26.00 ha	Pig– 10 nos.	10 nos		
	Fencing– 26 ha	26.00 ha			Poultry– 20 units	20 units		
6 SINANADI	Reclamation– 50 ha	50.00 ha	Reclamation– 10 ha	10.0 ha				
	Seeds – 16 q	16 q			(This project has been dropped since 1983-84)			
	Seedlings/ Grafts– 0.19 lakhs	0.19 lakhs						
	Fertiliser– 22 q	22 q						

continued................

TABLE II.3
Achievement on IJDP for the period 1982-83 to 1985-86

1	2	3	4	5	6	7	8	9	10
NORTH CACHAR HILLS DISTRICT									
1 AMRUDISA									
	Reclamation– 10 ha	8.00 ha	Reclamation– 55 ha	55.00ha	Seeds– 3.52 q	3.52 q	Speed–0.25 q	0.25 q	
	Improvement of jhum land 14 ha	14.00 ha	Ginger rhizome 22.50 q	22.50 q	Seedlings/ Grafts – 0.41 lakhs	0.41 lakhs	Seedlings/ Grafts – 0.40 lakhs	0.35 lakhs	
	Pig–12 units	12 units	Seedlings/ Grafts– 1.18 lakhs	1.18 lakhs	Ginger rhizome– 6q	6q	Ginger rhizome– 10.50 q	10.50 q	
			Pesticides 1.15 q	1.15 q	Heifer– 17 nos	17 nos.	Heifer–2nos.	2nos.	
					Goat–37 units	37 units	Goat–10 units	10 units	
			Sprayer 22 nos.	22 nos.			Pig– 8 units	8 Units	
					Duck – 29 units	29 units			
					Fishery tank– 6 nos	6 nos.			
			Small agricultural implements– 2 2 units	22 units	Charkha– 8 nos	8 nos.	Poultry– 20 units	20 units	

continued.........

1	2	3	4	5	6	7	8	9	10
2. INDRIMBUNGLOW									
		Reclamation– 4 ha Seedlings/Grafts– 0.79 lakhs Ginger rhizome– 40 q Small agricul– tural implements– 20 units	4.00 ha 0.79 lakhs 40 q 20 units	Reclamation– 13.61 ha Seedlings/Grafts 1.25 lakhs Ginger rhizome– 65 q Insecticides– 1.64 q and 10.00 ltrs	13.61 ha 1.25 lakhs 65 q 1.64 q 10.00 ltrs.	Reclamation– 20.96 ha Seeds 1.35 q Seedlings/Grafts 0.26 lakhs Ginger rhizome– 135 q	20.96 ha 1.35 q 0.26 lakhs 135 q	Reclamation– 13.42 ha Seeds - 0.40 q Seedlings/Grafts– 0.18 lakhs Ginger rhizome– 45.50 q	13.42 ha 0.40 q 0.18 lakhs. 45.50 q

Continued

TABLE II.3

Achievement on IJDP for the period 1982-83 to 1985-86

1	2	3	4	5	6	7	8	9	10
2	INDRIMBUNGLOW								
		Fertiliser– 20 q	20 q	Small agricultural implements– 24 units	24 units	Pesticides– 65 ltrs	65 ltrs	Small agricultural implements– 66 nos.	66 nos.
		Pesticides– 3 q	3 q	Sprayer – 24 nos.	24 nos.	Small/agricultural implements– 54 nos.	54 nos.	Sprayer– 1 no.	1 no.
				Fishery Tank– 3 nos.	3 nos.	Cow-15nos.	15 nos.	Heifer– ·13 nos.	13 nos.
						Goat-1 unit	1 unit	Goat - 1 unit	1 unit
						Pig - 2 units	2 units	Pig- 6 units	6 units
						Poultry- 4 units	4 units	Poultry– 2 units	2 units
						Fishery tank– 4 nos.	4 nos.	Fishery tank– 2 nos.	2 nos.
								Sewing machine- 4 nos.	4 nos.
								Cottage Industry– 2 units	2 units

continued...

1	2	3	4	5	6	7	8	9	10
3	BOROMOULKOI								
		Reclamation– 15.50 ha	15.50 ha	Reclamation– 64.32 ha	64.32ha	Reclamation– 50.55 ha	50.55 ha	Reclamation– 12 ha	11.91 ha
						Seeds– 2.50 q	2.50 q	Seeds - 30 q	30 q
		Terracing 0.31 ha	0.31 ha	Seedlings/Grafts– 4.30 lakhs	4.30 lakhs				
		Comp hut– 1 no.	1 no.	Ginger rhizome– 200 q	200 q	Seedlings/Grafts 1.06 lakhs	1.06 lakhs	Seedlings/Grafts 0.75 lakhs	0.75 lakhs
				Pesticides– 1.10 q and 10 ltrs	1.10 q 10 ltrs	Ginger rhizome– 300 q	300 q	Culvert – 2 nos.	2 nos.
						Fishery tank- 1 no.	1 no.	Sugarcane crusher– 4 nos.	4 nos.
				Sprayer– 15 nos.	15 nos.	Bullock– 42 nos.	42 nos.		
				Small agriculture implements– 45 units	45 units	Cow – 6 nos. Pig – 4 units	6 nos. 4 units		
						Poultry– 25 units	25 units		

TABLE II.3

Achievement on IJDP for the period 1982-83 to 1985-86

1	2	3	4	5	6	7	8	9	10
4	NATUN LEIKUL								
		Terracing– 3 ha	3.00 ha	Reclamation– 34.52 ha	34.52 ha	Reclamation– 26.37 ha	26.37ha	Reclamation– 35 ha	34.38 ha
		Reclamation– 6.80 ha	6.80 ha	Seeds– 51 q	51 q	Seeds – 75.85 q	75.85 q	Seeds – 135 q	134.55 q
		Bench terracing– 6.80 ha	6.80 ha	Seedlings/ Grafts– 4.42 lakhs	4.42 lakhs	Seedlings/ Grafts- 3.331 akhs	3.33 lakhs	Seedlings/ Grafts– 1 lakh	1.00 lakh

continued ....

1	*2*	*3*	*4*	*5*	*6*	*7*	*8*	*9*	*10*
4	NATUN LEIKUL								
		Half-moon terracing– 6.80 ha	6.80 ha	Ginger rhizome– 180 q	180 q	Ginger rhizome– 212 q	212 q	Ginger rhizome– 359q	358.50 q
		Seedlings/ Grafts– 1.75 lakhs	1.75 lakhs	Fertiliser–55q	55 q	Fencing– 800 R.M.	800 R.M.	Small agricultural implements – 249 nos.	249 nos.
				Pesticides-3 q	3 q				
				Fishery tank–1no.	1no.	Fishery tank– 5nos	5 nos.	5 H.P. Power pump– 1no.	1 no.
		Ginger rhizome– 12 q	12 q	Bullock-10nos.	10nos.	Bullock– 16 nos.	16 nos.	Heifer-33 nos.	33 nos.
				Pig –7 units	7 units	Cow – 11 nos.	11 nos.	Goat-46 units	46 units
				Poultry–12 units	12 units	Pig 10 units	10 units	Pig- 11 units	11units
		Extension of nalla- 5140 R.M.	5140 R.M.			Poultry– 30 units	30 units	Poultry – 12 units	12 units
		Fencing – 10100 R.M.	10100R.M.					Sewing machine- 16 nos.	16 nos.
								Cottage industry– 32 units	32units
								Eri & Mulberry rearer– 12 nos.	12 nos.

1	2	3	4	5	6	7	8	9	10
5 DIGENDU Pt IV									
		Reclamation– 11 ha	11.00 ha	Reclamation– 14 ha	14.00 ha	Seeds– 1 q	1 q	Reclamation– 13 ha	12.33 ha
		Improvement of jhum land– 16 ha	16.00 ha	Terrace – 6 ha	6.00 ha	Sugarcance crusher– 4 nos.	4 nos.	Seeds- 4 q	4 q
				Seeds – 14.50 q	14.50 q			Ginger rhizome 24 q	24 q
				Ginger rhizome 3 q	3.00 q 7 nos.	Sewing Machine 7 nos.	Seedlings/Grafts 0.01 lakhs	0.01 lakhs	
		Broad base terrace– 3 ha	3.00 ha	Seedlings/Grafts– 2.24 lakhs	2.24 lakhs	Bullock– 8 nos.	8 nos.	Heifer– 8 nos	8 nos.
				Irrigation channel– 1000 Mts.	1000 Mts.	Heifer 2nos.	2 nos.	Goat– 17 units	17units
				Farm forestry– 10 ha	10 ha	Poltry 12 units	12 units	Poultry– 13 units	13 units
				Pesticides – 3 q	3 q	Bullock cart- 2 nos.	2nos.	Sewing machine- 8 nos.	8 nos.

Source : Office of the Development Commissioner for the Hill Areas, Assam.

etc., have been supplied to the people of the villages for their economic uplift. The total number of animals and birds supplied to them is found to be 220. (iii) For the development of pisciculture, community fisheries have been provided under this programme. In addition, fish seeds, *kholihoi* (oil cakes), lime and rice bran etc., have also been supplied for utilisation in the community fisheries. (iv) Schemes relating to water harvest structures which involve erection of earthen dams are implemented for the purpose of minor irrigation, fishery and duckery etc., in the surveyed villages of the Karbi Anglong district. (v) In respect of cottage industries, it has been found that only 16 households of the villages have received assistance in the form of tailoring and carpentry. (vi) With regard to handloom and textiles, it is observed that yarns have been supplied for weaving clothes. Moreover, looms and accessories including corrugated iron sheets for making temporary sheds for weaving have been provided to certain villages like Harlongjuwe and Umcherra etc. (vii) The people of the villages have also received assistance in the form of coffee and rubber plantation assistance on community plots and horticultural seedlings and grafts viz., pineapple, banana, mango, plum, ginger, guava, black pepper, turmeric and citrus fruits etc., to improve their economic conditions. (viii) So far as agricultural inputs are concerned, it has been found that fertilizers like urea, super phosphate, MOP and chlorine powder etc., pesticides viz, anusar and various types of implements like spade, *dao,* sickle, fork and hand sprayer etc., have been provided to the people. The investigation reveals that as a result of implementation of the various schemes in the surveyed villages, the number of households engaged in shifting cultivation shows a decreasing trend. Out of the total number of 300 households of the selected villages, the number of households engaged in *jhum* just before starting of the programme was 257 i.e. 85.67% of the total households. After implementation of the welfare schemes it is seen that out of 257 *jhumia* households, 51 households (19.8%) have totally given up shifting cultivation. The remaining 206 households (80.2%) are, of course, practising it either partially or fully. In this connection, it is to be noted that during the time of field investigation the people were reported not to have received immediate benefits out of the various family-oriented and community-oriented schemes. As such, it is expected that the number of households leaving shifting cultivation would increase in the near future" (Das, 1997 : 238).

TABLE II.4

IJDP centres in Karbi Anglong and N.C. Hills

Sl. No.	*Name of the centre*	*Total households*	*Name of the centre*	*Total households*
1	*2*	*3*	*4*	*5*
	KARBI ANGLONG		**NORTH CACHAR HILLS**	
1	Dolamara	117	Hajong	29
2	Kaipani	60	Natun Disao	75
3	Kekang Adong	50	Semkhor	210
4	Thijoklangso	50	Motiriao Semdikhor	39
5	Rongnagar	39	Thunje Hereidalo	60
6	Rongbong Adong	45	Laisong	167
7	Rongpi Ronghang I	34	Moucher	32
8	Rongpi Ronghang II	23	Hange	49
9	Thekerajan	22	Lasang	54
10	Mugasong	29	Boro-Arkap	54
11	Phanglangso	70	Dimdao Wapu	34
12	Jilangso	96	Boro Langlai	22
13	Langlakso	200	Sangbar	100
14	Tikaklangso	50	Thuruk	38
15	Recho Apam	55	Khobak	50
16	Tharvecherop	67	Michidui	50
17	Langhonjar	48	Diblong	39
18	Kolonga Pathar	37	Choto Wapu	41
19	Engleng Merok	75	Gunjung	111
20	Menmiji	163	Amlangbra	40
	Total	1330		1294

N.B. : The last three centres from each district have been dropped from IJDP.

Under State Sector *Jhum* Control Programme also, 4 Mini Compact Areas viz., Hidipi and Miyungdisa in the Diphu subdivision of Karbi Anglong and Digerkuki in the Maibang subdivision and Jinam Valley in the Haflong subdivision of North Cachar Hills were identified as per suggestion of the Planning Commission in a meeting held on 4.9.89 in New Delhi and schemes were implemented from 1991-20 wjtb a project period of four years. Socio-economic surveys in respect of the above mentioned Mini Compact areas have been conducted by the Office of the District Research Officer, Karbi Anglong, Diphu in the year 1990 with a view to highlighting the prevailing socioenonomic condition of the people before implementation of the schemes under MCAP.

The study on Miyungdisa MCAP (Das, 1991) reveals that the Project Area covers sixteen villages with 196 households. "The total population is 1102 out of which males and females are 591 and 511 respectively. Sex ratio is per 1000 : 864. Interestingly, there are 3 villages where the females exceed males and the sex ratio is 1071, 1095 and 1307 per 1000 males. Transport and communication facilities are not satisfactory. There is only one motorable road running through the heart of the Project Area but due to non-availability of transport system, the people have to face difficulties. The distance of all the surveyed villages from the Block H.Q. located at Manja is more than 20 km. The location of the post office is within easy reach of the people in comparison to telegraph office. Three villages are located within 8 km. from the District H.Q., Diphu and therefore, the people of these villages may take better advantage of the facilities provided by the health institutions than the people of other villages of the Project Area. The total number of students coming from the selected villages to the primary schools in 1990 is 101 out of which male and female students are 65 (64.4%) and 36 (35.6%) respectively. On the other hand, out of 237 children in the age group 6-10 years, 101 children attend Primary Schools, the percentage being 42.6 only. The total number of students reading in M.E.Schools is 28 out of which the number of boys is 20 (71.4%) and that of the girls is 8 (28.6%) only. This indicates that a sharp decline in attendance to schools by the students after primary stage of education. Again, the number of students from these villages is 15 (Male = 13 and Female = 2) in High Schools only. Nobody is found to be reading in Higher Secondary or College level.This reveals that the people are still not very much aware of the importance of imparting formal education to their children. On the whole, literacy rate in the Project Area is 16.8% against 19.2% in the district

TABLE II.5

Villages under Hirhiri Barpanjan Watershed Management Project in Karbi Anglong

Sl. No.	*Name of the village*	*Total population*	*Total households*
1	*2*	*3*	*4*
1	Rongbong Ghat	115	20
2	Paisa Ingti	32	5
3	Langkhung Teron	184	30
4	Hirhiri Thengal	134	24
5	Hirhiri Pamai Killing	149	21
6	Majung Tokbi	52	9
7	Sarthe Rongphar	92	13
8	Lungtik Rongpi	18	3
9	Sarthe Tongpi	80	12
10	Sarthe Teron	86	13
11	Rongagora	188	27
12	Mensing Rongphar	144	17
13	Sikari Teron	19	3
14	Signot Ingti	81	15
15	Belu Ingti	58	13
16	Lindok Teron	24	4
17	Balphang Ingti	10	3
18	Amreng Ingti	62	10
19	Kather	87	10
20	Ram Lekthe	196	34
21	Paise	125	20
22	Anjak Ingti	54	8
23	Sarthe Tisso	60	10
	Total	2020	324

TABLE II.6

Villages under Chinthong CADP in Karbi Anglong

Sl. No.	*Name of the Village*	*Total households*	*Sl. No.*	*Name of the Villages*	*Total households*
1	*2*	*3*	*4*	*5*	*6*
1	Bodilangso	54	19	Socheng	33
2	Rongmandu	40	20	Langkarcha	29
3	Borpu	36	21	Langkaron	12
4	Lanqsomepi	57	22	Langmekang	22
5	Umphanchi	18	23	Changkup	18
6	Manjili	7	24	Sekphubang	27
7	Rongchek	81	25	Ujan Donka	68
8	Umdap	76	26	Habaigaon	29
9	Langteng	28	27	Langmet	51
10	Langtoi	36	28	Tirkim	44
11	Langparpam	72	29	Patorgaon	28
12	Ami	41	30	Umteli	23
13	Mujong	58	31	Harlong juwe	51
14	Umcherr	45	32	Arling	67
15	Amlong	66	33	Rangkor	57
16	Ambinong	9	34	Rumphum	36
17	Umrenti	27	35	Umphu	58
18	Longpai	66	36	Hamren Christian	18
	Total	817			671

Total hounseholds = 817 + 671 = 1488

TABLE II.7

Villages under Handingma CADP in North Cachar Hills

Sl. No.	*Name of the Village*	*Total households*	*Sl. No.*	*Name of the Villages*	*Total households*
1	*2*	*3*	*4*	*5*	*6*
1	Maibangsa	31	21	Choto Wapu	41
2	Deleisa	8	22	Dehangi	17
3	Jembru	34	23	Wari Longlabra	20
4	Guliabra	16	24	Jorai	23
5	Gajo	19	25	Disagutu	6
6	Lamadisa	40	26	Thaijupang	39
7	Amlangbra	40	27	Samaridisa	58
8	Thaimodoling	10	28	Moti Daodung	27
9	Hojai Dobonglong	18	29	Longmailai	19
10	Gunjung	123	30	Malao	23
11	Wari	31	31	Thaisilinghawar	40
12	Dersi	28	32	Hagjer	19
13	Naidingpur	20	33	Hojai	25
14	Gowaidisa	27	34	Riambathari	15
15	Thanalambra	14	35	Walaodisa	28
16	Lungkhok	43	36	Gurubari	25
17	Choto Longren	13	37	Riyao	25
18	Nanadisa	23	38	Disagism	13
19	Wayungdisa	13	39	Borlangdisa	18
20	Jorai Bathari	23	40	Ashrang	21
	Total	574			502

Total households = 574 + 502 = 1076

as per 1971 Census. There is no provision of drinking water in the form of piped water, tubewell or reservoir within the Project Area. The people have to depend on *katcha* well or natural spring and river for which they are likely to suffer from various water-borne diseases. The weekly/daily markets are located at a distance not easily accessible to the people. As a result, they have to purchase daily necessities at exorbitant rate from the grocery shops (15 nos.), located in and around the selected villages. Out of the total number of 196 households, 159 (81.1%), 67 (34.1%) and 72 (36.7%) are engages in weaving, bamboo & cane works and sericulture respectively. These cottage industries which are practised by the people from generation to generation may be modernised by means of executing suitable schemes by the Government agencies for large scale production. Otherwise the cottage industries cannot be expected to play any significant role in improving the socio-economic condition of the people.

98.47% of the total households practise cultivation as the primary occupation. Only 1.02% of the households are in service while a negligible percentage of households (0.51%) have adopted business as primary occupation. This indicated that the people of the Project Area are entirely dependent on agriculture and there is hardly any noticeable change among them in case of acceptance of non-agrarian occupation as the primary source of livelihood. The field investigation reveals that out of 196 households, 103 (52.5%) depend mainly on daily wage earning in or outside their habitat and this reveals that complete dependence on primary occupation by the people is not at all possible. The percentage of workers in the Project Area is found to be 59.3.

The total area of land possessed by the households is 4290 *bighas* out of which the area of land under cultivation is 3427 *bighas,* i.e. 79.88% of the total amount of land. Moreover, homestead land, fishery and fallow land cover 320 *bighas* (7.46%), 15 *bighas* (0.35%) and 528 *bighas* (12.3%) respectively. It may be mentioned here that out of 3427 *bighas* of cultivable land, the total area of land under *jhum* and settled cultivation is 1503 *bighas* (43.85%) and 1924 *bighas* (56.14%) respectively. It transpires from this analysis that besides settled cultivation the people of the Project Area do practise *jhum* extensively. The average land-holding per household and per capita land-holding in the selected villages of the Project Area are 21.8 *bighas* and 3.8 *bighas* respectively. The rate of production of paddy from *jhum* land and settled mode of cultivation is found to be 1.9 quintals and 2.3 quintals per *bigha* respectively. Only ten households (5.1%)

possess fisheries covering 15 *bighas* of land. The type of fishery may be classified into tank (9 nos.), *beel* (2 nos.) and channel (2 nos.). The amount of expenditure incurred on fishery in the year 1989 is Rs.5300.00. On the other hand, the quantity of fish caught in the fisheries is 7 quintals 88 kilograms, the approximate value of which accounts for Rs.12800.00. The people of the Project Area possess livestock. Bullocks numbering 368 constitute 9.39% and cows numbering 82 constitute 2.09% of the total livestock population. The number of poultry is 2413, the percentage being 61.56. There are also 645 pigs and 406 goats which account for 16.45% and 10.36% respectively. Out of sixteen villages, buffaloes are found in two villages. The number of buffaloes is 6 (0.15%) only.

In bygone days the Karbis used to shift their houses from one place to another in search of *jhum* land. They did not consider it necessary to preserve important household properties. Their life-style was very simple. Since every society is dynamic in nature, some changes have also taken place among the people of the Project Area. The investigation reveals that there are 34 bicycles, 4 tape-recorders, 73 radios, 30 guns, 45 watches and one television in the selected villages. The traditional housing pattern which is known as pile dwelling has also undergone changes. Except one pile dwelling house, the remaining 368 thatched houses are constructed on grounds. However, Assam Type or R.C.C. building is not observed in the Project Area.

The average gross annual income of a household is estimated at Rs.14,771.32. On the other hand, the average annual expenditure of a household is found to be Rs.13,650.16. As a result, the average household is found to have possessed a very insignificant surplus budget amounting to Rs.1,121.16. Per capita annual expenditure is found to be Rs. 2,427.80 against per capita annual income of Rs.2,627.20. This shows that per capita surplus is Rs.199.40 only per annum. In short, it may be said that the pattern of livelihood of the people inhabiting the Project Area is not satisfactory and their economy is still at subsistence level, having only a marginal surplus.

It may be mentioned here that out of a total of 196 households, 90 (45.9%) are in the habit of taking loans for the purpose of solving their problems which mainly consist of maintenance of family and operation of agricultural activities etc. The investigation reveals that except one household who has taken loan amounting to Rs.500.00 from the DRDA,

Diphu, other households approach the village people, *mahajans* or shopkeepers etc., for obtaining loan, either in cash or in kind. It is seen that 0.13%, 17.46% and 82.11% of the total amount of loan are taken from DRDA, village people including *mahajans* and shopkeepers respectively. The rate of interest is found to be 10% per annum in respect of loan from DRDA. On the contrary, the rate of interest is much higher in case of loan availed from other sources. Normally, the people have to pay 10-20% interest per month. In some cases, the rate of interest is fixed at 50% per annum. The average debt per household is estimated at Rs.590.00 and the average debt per indeleted house hold is worked out to be Rs.1,285.00. It may, therefore, be assumed that indebtedness has a deleterious effect on the economy of the people".

Furthermore, two Compact Areas viz., Samelangso-Rongmongve in Karbi Anglong and Mahur-Laisong Road-Maibang (East) in North Cachar Hills and six Mini Compact Areas viz., Socheng, Amri and Nilip in Karbi Anglong and Diyungmukh-Dehangi, Mahur and Mupa-Langting in North Cachar Hills were identified for implementation of the schemes. The office of the District Research Officer, Diphu has also undertaken socio-economic surveys in Samelangso-Rongmongve CADP (60 villages) and Mahur-Laisong Road-Maibang (East) CADP (44 villages) in 1992. Moreover, the establishment has carried out socio-economic surveys in Socheng MCAP (20 villages) and Diyungmukh-Dehangi MCAP (26 villages) in the year 1993 and Mahur MCAP (26 villages) and Mupa-Langting MCAP (24 villages) in the year 1994. Major findings of the Report of the survey of socio-economic condition of the people of Samelangso-Rongmongve CADP are furnished below:

1. The Samelangso-Rongmongve Compact Area of Karbi Anglong district is mainly inhabited by the Karbis. There are altogether sixty villages within the Project Area. The total number of households is 1,196 and the total population is 6,849. Sex ratio is 1000 : 932.

2. The number of villages located within 0-3 km. and 4-7 km. from the nearest motorable road is 19 (31.67%) and 22 (36.67%) respectively. Other villages are more than 7 km. away from the nearest motorable road. Only three villages are located at a distance of 4/5 km from the nearest railway station.

3. The location of the post office is wihtin easy reach of the people in comparison to that of telegraph office. Thirty villages (50%) are at a

distance of 0-5 km. from the nearest post office. On the contrary, three villages (5%) are located from the nearest telegraph office in the same range.

4. 37 villages (61.67%) are found to be located at a distance of 0-5 km from the nearest medical institutions. Other villages are more than 5 km away from the nearest medical institutions.

5. The number of L.P., M.E. and H.E. Schools in and around the Project Area is 34, 9 and 6 respectively. During the year 1992, the numbers of students attending Primary, Middle and High Schools from the Project Area are found to be 721, 277 and 225 respectively. College-going students are thirteen only.

6. The percentage of literacy in the Project Area is 27.89. For spread of education, more educational institutions should be established.

7. Drinking water facilities are not satisfactory in the Project Area. People use to take water from *katcha* or *pucca* well, pond, river and natural spring. Tubewells are found in four villages only. Similarly, tap water facilities are available in four villages.

8. Out of sixty villages, 20 (33.33%) are located at a distance of 0-6 km from the nearest weekly market. The remaining villages are more than 6 km away from the nearest weekly market. There are three Fair Price shops and eleven other shops within the Project Area. The LAMPS established at Nilip, Deithor Kekang Adong, Silonijan, Rongmongve and Rongagora help the people in getting essential commodities.

9. Out of the total number of 1,196 households, the number of households engaged in weaving, bamboo and cane works and sericulture is found to be 856 (71.57%), 675 (56.4%) and 189 (15.8%) respectively. The people are least conscious for adopting these cottage industries on commercial level.

10. The number of households having cultivation, service and business as primary occupation is 1,111 (92.89%), 40 (3.34%) and 10 (0.84%) respectively. Moreover, 35 households (2.93%) are found to be adopting daily wage as the primary source of occupation for their livelihood. Out of 1,196 household, 369 (30.85%) have secondary occupation. Workers constitute 54.21% against 45.79% of non-workers in the Project Area.

11. Out of the total households of 1,196, the number of households having land in the categories 0-11 *bighas* and 12-23 *bighas* is 670 (56.02%) and 373 (31.19%) respectively. Only 153 households (12.79%) possess land in the category of 24 *bighas* and above. The total area of land possessed by the people is 16,330 *bighas* out of which the areas of land under *jhum,* wet, horticulture, homestead, fallow land and fishery are 3,547 *bighas* (36.96%), 6,051 *bighas* (63.04%), 3,560 *bighas* (21.8%), 2,484 *bighas* (51.21%) 631 *bighas* (3.25%) and 157 *bighas* (0.96%) respectively.The average landholding per household is 13.7 *bighas.* Per capita land-holding is 2.4 *bighas.* The rate of production of paddy is 1.45 quintals per bigha in jhum and 2.11 quintals per bigha in wet cultivation.

12. The number of livestock population in the Project Area is 14,015. Poultry, pigs and goats constitute 55.24%, 13.27% and 10.95% respectively. Bullocks account for 11.21% against 9.33% of cows.

13. Among the household properties mention may be made of bicyle (533 nos.), watch (281), vehicle (13), tape-recorder (86), radio (380), television (9) and gun (64) etc. Moreover, residential houses are of the following types: Pile dwelling (53), thatched (1,731), *katcha* Assam Type (133), *pucca* A.T. (7) and R.C.C. (1).

14. The people of the Project Area derive 70.17% of income from land, 21.24% from paid employment including daily wage, 3.67% from trade & commerce, 2.36% from cottage industry, 2.17% from livestock and 0.39% from fishery.The average gross annual income of a household is found to be Rs. 11,397.59. Per capita annual income is Rs. 1,987.15.

15. The major head of expenditure is food which accounts for 57.7% of the total expenditure. The people use to spend 6.86% in dress and ornaments, 5.44% in kerosene, toilet and utensil, 5.05% in beverage, tobacco and betelnut, 4.93% in education and 4.09% in health. The average annual expenditure per household is Rs.9,023.75. Per capita expenditure is Rs.1.575.76. The average household has a marginal surplus budget of Rs.2,355.84. Per capita surplus is worked out to be Rs.411.39 per annum.

IJDP & The Present Study

Keeping all these antecedents, tacts, views and observations in mind, in the present study, it has been intended to take up a detailed intensive investigation of some selected centres in Karbi Anglong to attempt an objective assessment and understanding of the impact of the different schemes under the programme on the Karbis.

As noted earlier, there are in all seventeen centres under the IJDP. Out of these, a total of ten centres have conveniently been selected for the purpose of the present study.

The broad objectives of the study will be as follows:

(i) To have a detailed idea of the different schemes under the programme as well as their mode of implementation in the studied centres.

(ii) To have an assessment of the prevailing state of affairs with regard to the co-ordination between the potential beneficiaries and the implementing agency/personnel.

(iii) People's attitude towards the age-old practice of shifting cultivation vis-a-vis the alternative permanent mode of livelihood.

(iv) To have an idea about the difference (if any) in the extent of *jhum* cultivation before and after implementation of the programme.

(v) Beneficiaries' views with regard to their overall economic condition before and after implementation of the programme.

(vi) To have an overall assessment of the impact of the programme on the life of the Karbis.

The study will be guided by the lone hypothesis, "the IJDP has taken care of all relevant aspects and is being accepted by the people without leading to a social disorganization".

Methodology

It has already been mentioned that the number of IJDP centres in the Karbi Anglong district of Assam is seventeen and these are exclusively inhabited by the hill Karbis. Out of these centres, 10 (ten) centres have been selected for the study on the basis of random sampling. Necessary schedules have been prepared for collecting primary data. Interview schedules have been administered to each household, preferabley the head of household of the selected centres. Moreover, important particulars in relation to each centre viz., location, transport and communication system, civic and educational facilities and other basis amenities are recorded in a separate schedule. Case histories are also collected from several beneficiaries to assess the impact of the programme on the people. Furthermore, group interviews have been carried out in all the studied centres since the programme covered community oriented schemes. Attempts have also been made to understand the various dimensions of the programme through personal observation. As a part of participant observation method night halts have been made in some households of the centres to establish good rapport with the people for understanding their emic views towards settled mode of cultivation as well as shifting cultivation.

The study has been carried out between April, 1993 and January, 1995. After completion of field work, tabulation and analysis of data have been taken up from the early part of 1996 by applying standard statistical methods. Secondary data have been collected from different sources viz., Government departments, District Council offices, research journals, books and newspapers etc. The mass of data thus collected have been systematically arranged and presented in several chapters in the dissertation. In addition, photographs relating to the programme as well as various aspects of life and culture of the Karbis have also been incorporated in the dissertation as far as practicable. Furthermore, necessary maps, graphs and statistical tables have been included into the relevant chapters of the discourse.

The entire mass of data has conveniently been presented in seven chapters.

The *First Chapter (Introduction)* provides an idea about the practice of shifting cultivation in general and that in Karbi Anglong in particular. The chapter also attempts a brief review of available literatures dealing with the studies carried out on different aspects of shifting cultivation.

While dealing with *The Problem* in the *Second Chapter* a detailed discussion has been made on the various developmental projects contemplated and implemented in the two hill districts (Karbi Anglong and North Cachar Hills) of Assam. The findings of the various evaluation studies carried out by different agencies and individuals have also been incorporated here. The purpose and the area of the present study, too, have been introduced in this chapter.

A brief ethnographic note on the Karbis, the population under study has been attempted in the *Third Chapter (The Karbis)*.

The *Fourth Chapter (The Field)* provides a brief introduction on the land and the people where the present study has been carried out.

A reasonably detailed idea about different schemes under the development programme as well as potential beneficiaries involved in it has been provided in the *Fifth Chapter (The Economic Profile of the People and the Programme)*.

The *Sixth Chapter* deals with the observed and assessed impact of the programme on the people involved in it.

Finally, the *Seventh Chapter* (*Summary and Conclusion*) summarises the entire work that also incorporates some relevant concluding remarks.

III

THE KARBIS

The Karbis, formerly known as the Mikirs constitute a major tribe in the autonomous hill district of Karbi Anglong, Assam. Some of their brethren are found to settle sparsely in several districts of the State viz., North Cachar Hills, Nagaon, Morigaon, Golaghat, Sonitpur, Lakhimpur and Kamrup etc. Moreover, their settlements are known in Nagaland, Meghalaya, Manipur and Arunachal Pradesh. It is often heard that the Karbis are living in Sylhet of Bangladesh and Myanmar also.

According to 1971 Census the total Karbi population in Karbi Anglong and North Cachar Hills is 1,72,845 and 4,349 respectively. It is to be noted that the Karbis are not scheduled in the plains districts of Assam and as a result, the number of population living therein is not available from the census records. The Karbis constitute 1.21% and 11.03% of the total population and the total scheduled tribe population of the State respectively. The rate of literacy among them is 13.18%, the male and female literacy rates being 21.09 and 4.95 respectively, as per 1971 Census.

Affinity

Like all other tribes of Assam the Karbis also belong to the Mongoloid group. Linguistically they are included in the Tibeto-Burman branch of the Sino-Tibetan group. They constitute an "interesting tribe in the sense that though they belong to Assam-Burma group of the Tibeto-Burman linguistic family they can neither be put under Bodo nor any other linguistic group. Grierson (1904) classified them as an intermediate group between the Bodo and the Western Naga on the basis of language. Again, some others want to suggest that Karbi language shows mixture of Austric and Bodo languages, though they undoubtedly belong to the Tibeto-Burman linguistic family. According to some scholars the Karbi language has some similarities with certain Naga dialects on the one hand and Lushai-Kuki dialects on the other" (Kar, 1994 : 10).

While discussing the place of the karbis in the Tibeto-Burman linguistic family Lyall (1971 : 153) observes, "Ever since the race has been studied, it has been noticed that it was difficult to establish its exact place and affinities in the heterogeneous congeries of peoples who inhabit the mountainous region between India and Burma. This was remarked by Robinson in 1841 and 1849, by Stewart in 1855, by Damant in 1879. During the census of 1881 an attempt was made to bring the Mikirs into relation with the Boro or Kachari stock; but it was then realised that more must be ascertained regarding their neighbours before any final judgement could be arrived at. Dr. Grierson, on linguistic grounds, has classed them in the *Linguistic Survey* as intermediate between the Boro and the Western Nagas. It appears in the light of much fuller information were available, that they should be classed rather with these tribes which form the connecting link between the Nagas and the Kuki-Chins, and that the preponderance of their affinities lies with the latter of these two races, especially those dwelling in the south of the Arakan Roma range, where the Chin tends to merge into the Burman of the Irawadi Valley".

On the basis of the ballads prevalent among the Karbis, Kathar (1988 : 4) maintains, "According to the oral history of the tribe, the Karbis once lived together with the Kuki-Chins. In the ballad *Musera,* the Kuki-Chins were referred to by a singular name *Kuki Chindaipo.* This ballad is, in fact, the ancient history of the Karbis. The other ballads from which portions of the history of the Karbis can be derived are the ballads of framing of rules for marriage ceremony, discovery of rice etc. All these ballads point to the fact that the Karbis are closely related to the Kuki-Chins. And the Karbi language belongs to the Kuki-Chin sub-group. It is, therefore, not correct to describe the Karbis as of Bodo origin. The Karbi language is also very closely related to the Naga-Kuki class of languages. Philologically the Karbi language has many similarities with the Ao, Angami and Tangkhul Nagas as well. For example, in counting, the Karbi and the Ao Naga languages are the same upto 6. For *dao* the Karbis call *nopak.* In the Ao it is *anok.* Both the Aos and the Karbis teach their kids to say *kak-kak* for no more. However, the closest affinities of Karbi language is found in the Kuki-Chin sub-group of languages..."

The Karbis do not have their own script. But they are rich in folklore. Terang (1982) remarks, "The stream of Karbi life is packed with the ingredients of folklore. Like any other culturally distinct ethnic group, the Karbi society also fondly cherishes almost all aspects of folklore including myths, tales, proverbs, charms, riddles, lays, ballads, dances, ceremonies and art etc."

Origin and Migration

It has already been mentioned that the Karbis were previously known as the Mikirs. But this name was given to them by some other community. "They call themselves *Arleng,* the meaning of which is 'slanting place near a hill, and thus denotes the people living in the slopes of the hills. Though many scholars use the term Arleng as equivalent to the word 'man', actually the *Manit* or *Munet* is the proper term used by the Karbi to denote a person. In fact, the word Arleng is confined to the men of Karbi tribe only. Now-a-days they identify themselves as Karbi, though the origin of the term is uncertain" (Medhi, 1988 : 8).

There are various legends with regard to the terms Mikir and Karbi. Out of them, only one legend each in respect of the terms is furnished here. Once upon a time, some tribal people were searching for their pet cat lost in the jungle. In the mean time, some people of other community met them and asked about their identity. The tribal people who were in search of the cat could not understand the language of those people but said that they were looking for their lost cat i.e., *Mengkiri* (*Meng* = cat, *kiri* = to search). From that day these people were known as *Mengkiri* which, later on, became *Mikir.* While discussing about the legend relating to the term Karbi Bordoloi (1985 : 56) observes, "The son of Barlia, one of their forefathers had once suffered from a very serious illness. Barlia worshipped *Hemphu*, the powerful family deity, for the recovery of his son by sacrificing some goats and fowls. When the worshipping was over, his daughter-in-law who was pregnant at that time, had suddenly developed labour pain. *Hemphu* instructed *Panjak*, a demoness to help the daughter- in–law in her delivery. *Panjak* obeyed accordingly. But unfortunately at the feast offered by *Barlia* no food could be offered to the *Panjak* since she was hiding herself from the glaring eyes of the guests. This fact came to the notice of *Hemphu* only when the serving of food was almost over. *Hemphu* then offered a portion of his food and the other guests also followed the suit. Giving something from one's plate is called *Thekar* and it is still prevalent in all worships. The people, therefore, introduced themselves as *Thekar Kibi Ache*. It is believed that the term Karbi is a derivation from *Thekar Kibi* ."

The original home of the Karbis is believed to be the Western China near the rivers Yang-te-Kiang and the Howang-ho. Later on, they moved along the courses of the rivers Chindwin and Irrawaty and reached Burma and settled there for a short period. Afterwards they entered into erstwhile Assam through the North-eastern route.

The traditional stories of migration are prevalent among the KARBIS. Once they lived on the banks of the Kopili and Kalong rivers and in and around the present National Park Kaziranga. But the Kachari kings drove them to the hills and as a result, they settled in the Jaintia kingdom. However, a section of the people crossed the Barapani river and lived in the Rongkhong hills establishing the capital at Socheng. On the other hand, due to constant attacks by the Jaintia kings the Karbis living therein migrated northward and lived within the Ahom kingdom. Unfortunately due to Burmese invasion they again proceeded to lower Assam and some of them went to the north bank crossing the river Brahmaputra. In course of time the capital established at Socheng was shifted to Niz Rongkhong located at Hamren.

Taking into consideration the traditional stories of migration Das (1987 : 49) comments, "............ perhaps they first made their settlement in the eastern region of the Khasi and Jayantia Hills. But for some reasons they could not go along well with the latter. Therefore, they moved to the Kachari kingdom and reached Dimapur. There too, they could not live in amity with the Kacharis for a longer time. They had to move again. Thus the stories suggest that the Karbis being surrounded by the Khasi, Kachari and the Naga were pushed from one place to another within a limited territory at different times before finally settling in Karbi Anglong. Therefore, they came in contact with different tribal groups from whom they picked up certain cultural elements including language".

Social Organisation

The Karbis living in the hills are divided into three groups. These are *Chinthong*, *Ronghang* and *Amri*. "However, these groups or sections do not indicate true tribal division supposed to be derived from common ancestors and united in blood. These names in all probability refer to their habitats. *Amri* seems to be a Khasi river name and *Ronghang* is the legendary site of the Sot Recho capital" (Dutt, 1979 : 73). Moreover, Devi (1992 : 183) opines, "The first two *(Chinthong and Ronghang)* rank rather higher than the third, because, it is said that the *Amri* excused themselves from sending a man to the Ahom king in Sibasagar, when a representative was required from each of the three sections of the tribe. Hence the *Amri* is excluded from sharing the liquor at a sacrifice and are held in contempt by the western Mikirs specially". Again, the Karbis living in the plains districts are known as *Dumrali* or *Thalua*.

The Karbis have five clans *(Kur)* viz., *Teron, Inghi, Ingti, Terang* and *Timung*. All the clans are socially equal in status. Each clan is again divided into several subclans. (Teron) (1974 : 7) provides the details of the sub-clans as follows :

Teron : (i) *Kongkat* (ii) *Langne* (iii) *Milik* (iv) *Ai* (v) *Chir-Ang and* (vi) *Trop Inghi:* (i) *Inghi* (ii) *Rongpi* (iii) *Ronghang* (iv) *Tisso* (v) *Hanse* (vi) *Lekthe* (vii) *Ke-ap* (viii) *Bongrung* (ix) *Kramsa* (x) *Rongpi Amri* (xi) *Rongpi Chinthong* (xii) *Rongpi Ronghang* (xiii) *Rongpi Lindok* (xiv) *Rongpi Miji* (xv) *Ronghi* (xvi) *Rongchehon* (xvii) *Rongo* (xviii) *Kete* (xix) *Kereng* (xx) *Kelum* (xxi) *Durong* (xxii) *Tisso Rongphu* (xxiii) *Tisso Rongling* (xxiv) *Tisso Mothou* (xxv) *Tisso Rongchi* (xxvi) *Tisso Rongchecho* (xxvii) *Hanse Chinthong* (xxvii) *Hanse Nongpip* (xxix) *Hanse Lindok and* (xxx) *Ronghang Lindok Ingti :* (i) *Ingti Kathar* (ii) *Ingti Henchek* (iii) *Taro* (iv) *Ingleng and* (v) *Ingti Killing Terang:* (i) *Terang Dili* (ii) *Terang Rongchecho* (iii) *Kro* (iv) *Be-dum* (v) *Be Ke-et and* (vi) *Be Ke-ik. Timung :* (i) *Timung* (ii) *Rongphar* (iii) *Singnar* (iv) *Tokbi* (v) *Phangcho* (vi) *Killing* (vii) *Timung Phura* (viii) *Timung (Rongpi* (ix) *Timung Killing* (x) *Tok Tiki* (xi) *Singnar Miji* (xii) *Singnar Pator* (xiii) *Tokbi Dera* (xiv) *Dera* (xv) *Kleng Rongphar* (xvi) *Rongphar Phura* (xvii) *Rongphar Ronghang* (xviii) *Phangcho Juiti (xix) Phangcho Langterois (xx) Phangcho Ingnar* (xxi) *Phangcho Wojaroo* (xxii) *Sengar Musiki (xxiii) Mu Sophi (xxiv) Nokbare* (xxv) *Sengnot* (xxvi) *Salut Sengnot* (xxvii) *Tokbi Chinthong* (xxviii) *Tokbi Ronghang* (xxix) *Nongdu and* (xxx) *Nonglada.*

They maintain clan exogamy. Marriage between members of the same clan is strictly prohibited. All the members of a clan are treated as brothers and sisters. Heavy punishment of excommunication is awarded to those who violate this social norm. Violation of the 'clan exogamy' rule is considered to be a social crime and is locally known as Laisenam. In this context it may be pointed out that marriage is not held etween *Teron* and *Ingti* since they consider themselves to belong to the same family, but a boy of *Milik* sub-clan of *Teron* clan can marry an *Ingti* girl. The reasons for this restriction as well as the partial relaxation, however, could not be ascertained.

Monogamy is the usual rule among the people. Cross-cousin marriage (mother's brother's daughter) is highly preferred. Divorce with the approval of the village council and widow remarriage can take place in the society. Junior levirate is practised. Bride price is practically absent among the people. Child marriage is also not practised. Marriage by negotiation is the most common practice among them. There are mainly four phases involved in the performance of a marriage *(Adamasar)*. Firstly, preliminary discussion is held between the two parties *(Nengpi Nengso Kachingki)*. Secondly, proposals are sent to the girl's parents for getting the girl *(Piso Kehang or kehang Ahar)*. Final settlement of marriage *(Lam Kepathik or Lam Athir Kebi)* takes place in the third phase. In this phase it is also decided whether the bridegroom will serve in the father-in-law's house after marriage for a specific period which means a marriage by service *(Akemen)*. If the bride–groom does not stay, the marriage is known as *Akejo*. In the fourth and final phase, the date for solemnisation of the marriage is fixed *(Ajo-Ari-Kepha)*.

It is interesting to note that among the Karbis the wife does not change her surname obtained by birth. For example, a girl having the surname *Teronpi* married to a *Timung* will not change her surname to *Timungpi* but her children born out of wedlock will assume the surname of their father i.e. boys will be *Timung* and girls *Timungpi.* The suffix 'pi' denotes females.

The Karbis are a patrilocal, patrilineal and patripotestal tribe. The girl after marriage goes to her husband's home and resides there. Generally, father is the head of the family. Sons inherit property after the death of the father. In absence of sons the nearest male relatives of the deceased inherit the same. In fact, the father distributes the land equally among his sons before his death. Although daughters have not right on the father's property they receive mother's property such as ornaments, clothes etc., equally. Adoption is not found among them.

Both nuclear and joint family systems are prevalent among the people. However, the nuclear families are numerically more than the joint families in the villages. The Report on the study of Miyungdisa Mini Compact Area Project (Das, 1991) reveals that the project Area comprising sixteen villages with 196 families had 148 nuclear families (75.5%) and 48 joint families (24.5%). Another Report on the study of Hidipi Mini Compact Area Project (Das, 1991) shows that the Project Area consisting of twelve villages with 239 families has 166 nuclear families (69.5%) and 73 joint families (30.5%). It has also been found in a Report on the study of Samelangso-Rongmongva Compact Area Project (Das, 1992) that out of a total of 1196 households inhabiting sixty villages, the number of nuclear families was 900 (75.25%) while that of joint families 296 (24.75%). "A survey conducted by the District Statistics Office, Diphu in 1964 revealed that the average size of a family was 5.93 in the district (then U.M. & N.C. Hills) and the average size of family in respect of the Mikkir Hills Division was found to be 6.26" (Pegu, 1980 : 201). In the present study the average size of family is found to be 5.38 only. It is thus apparent that the frequency of the joint family (at least structurally) is gradually decreasing among the people.

The Household

The characteristic feature of a traditional Karbi village is the smallness in it size. Few households constitute a village. Each village is usually named after the *Gaonbura* (headman). The village is preferably established on the hill slope/top. However, with the passage of time, many villages have been established in the plains areas. Although the traditional housing pattern of the Karbis is pile dwelling *(hemthengsong)*, at present, most of the people construct houses on the grounds *(hemlongle)*. The various parts of a pile dwelling house have been nicely described by Barkataki (1969 : 53) in this manner, "Houses are built of split , flattened out bamboo, the roof being thatched with *sun-grass.* The house is divided into separate compartments. A partition *(arpong)* running longitudinally divides it into two main parts. The one on the left is called *kut,* where the paddy is stored and the inmates of the family also sleep here. There is also a fire-place in it. The other part is called *kam* has which is meant for guests. The *kut* has only one door, while the *kam* has a door in front and another at the back. There are two fire-places in the *kam*. In this room on a platform or *chang (called tibung)*, at a level higher than the floor, they keep their water-*chungas* (bamboo-*tubes*). There is a verandah in the front *(hongkup)* and another at the back *(pang-hongkup)* beyond which there is an unroofed platform *(pang)*. On the left-hand side of the *kut* a portion with its floor at a lower level is partitioned off for the fowl and goat *(vo roi)*. *Damtak* in the *kut* is where the members sleep and the paddy is stored. Behind the fire-place in the middle of the *kut* is the *dam-buk* where the grown up children sleep. *Theng-poi-roi* is the place for storing fire-wood. In large houses a space is provided for guests to spend the night *(hong–pharla)*. The platform of the house is reached by the *don-don* at the right".

Normally, a Karbi family possesses the following household tools and implements for their day-to day use.

Anchoho	–	small measuring basket, generally used for cooking rice
Anlumphlak	–	spoon for distributing boiled rice
Anphule	–	utensil for cooking rice
Anthong	–	wooden saucepan for keeping boiled rice
Beleng	–	winnowing-tray
Bongchin	–	utensil made of pumpkin for carrying rice beer
Bongkari	–	water vessel with a spout
Bongkok	–	container made of big size pumpkin for keeping water
Burup	–	basket with a narrow neck used for keeping fish or dried chilli
Chir	–	hunting spear
Cho	–	axe
Chobak	–	large wooden spoon for distributing rice
Choklet	–	fishing implement
Dobor	–	utensil for keeping betel nut and leaf
Hak	–	bamboo basket having four legs without lid used for carrying paddy and other objects
Han lumphlak	–	spoon for distributing curry
Hatan	–	measuring basket
HIjap	–	fan made of bamboo
Horbong	–	Container made of-gourd with tapering mouth for keeping rice bear
Inghoi		wooden stool
IngKrung	–	sieve

Kilat	–	drinking glass
Kasu	–	dish
Kasu rahap	–	shelf for keeping dish
Ku	–	spade
Langbong	–	pitcher
Langpong	–	bamboo pipe for bringing water
Lengpum	–	pestle
Long	–	mortal
Mehip	–	fire-place
Nohirangso	–	sickle
Nok	–	sword
Nokanti	–	different form of *dao*
Nopak	–	dao
Noksu	–	small knife
Tar	–	sleeping mat
Thai	–	bow
Thaiaso	–	arrow
Therang	–	loom

Besides, some of the Karbi families possess guns with proper licence from the Deputy Commissioner's office. Moreover, at present, some of them possess watch, bicycle, radio, newspaper and television etc.

Economic Organisation

Agriculture is the primary occupation of the Karbis. They practise *jhuming* in the hilly areas and wet cultivation in the low lying areas. Terrace cultivation has also been recently introduced. The Karbis rear cattle, pigs and poultry etc. Bamboo and cane products are meant for household purpose only and not for sale. Women are found to be more laborious than the menfolk. Besides domestic works, they remain engaged in agricultural activities practically throughout the year. But the economic condition of the people does not seem to be very satisfactory. In *jhuming* they get minimum yield with maximum labour. Consumption of rice beer (*Horlang* and *Hor Arok)* leads to the utilisation of a huge portion of paddy. For most of the people, land alienation and indebtedness are almost a part of their life. Das (1987 : 181) comments, "...... among the Karbis, the tendency to lease their land for fixed produce is so great that most families even though they are otherwise capable of doing good cultivation, resort to frequent and regular mortgaging, despite the abolition of the *paikas* system in the area. Our study of 200 families have revealed that 80 per cent of the Karbis are involved in *paikas* system of mortgaging and indebtedness". In another survey conducted in five Karbi villages inhabited by 430 Karbi and 72 non–tribal families and located within the jurisdiction of the Howraghat Development Block of Karbi Anglong district, Bordoloi (1991 : 260) observes, "43.48 percent or 187 families have alienated 859.62 acres of land mainly in the forms of *Paikas, Khoi Bandhak* and *Adhi*. There are some cases of sale, *Sukti Bandhak* and encroachment also. The alienated land constitutes 30.79 per cent of the total landholdings of the scheduled tribe families in the five villages and also constitutes 61.70 per cent of the total landholdings of the land alienator families. In these five villages no land is found to have been acquired for public purposes. The area of alienated land from tribals to tribals is found to be 386.31 acres involving 106 Karbi families. The alienated land constitutes 13.83% of the total landholdings of the scheduled tribe families under the purview of the survey and 27.71% of the total landholdings of the land alienated families. Since transfer of land, whether be it of temporary or permanent nature, from tribals to tribals is not prohibited by the existing land laws of the Karbi Anglong District Council, alienation of 386.31 acres of land from tribals to tribals is not illegal. In this case the families involved constitute 24.65% of the total scheduled tribe families in the five villages. Our main concern is, however, with the transfer of land from tribals to non-tribals. It is found that 81 tribal families (18.83% of the total families) have alienated 473.31 acres of their land to non–tribals. The alienated land constitutes 16.96 per cent of the total landholdings of the Karbi families in the five villages and 33.98% of the landholdings of the land-alienated families of the five surveyed villages. The magnitude of the problem can be understood from the fact that the alienated land from tribals to non-tribals constitutes 64.33% of the total landholdings of 81 Karbi families. In other words these families have under their possession only 35.67% of their landholdings for self cultivation making the families almost landless".

Rongker and *Hacha Kekan* are the main agricultural festivals performed by the Karbis. Rongker is celebrated before the beginning of cultivation by worshipping various deities for the welfare of the people inhabiting the village concerned. The people sacrifice animals and birds in order to appease the deities so that they get rid of diseases and other natural disasters. Moreover, they expect to reap a good harvest without destruction of crops by wild animals and birds during the year. Entry of women into the worship area is strictly prohibited. "There is another kind of Rongker performed on a greater scale. This type of *Rongker* which is performed at the beginning of every five years is called *Wofong Rongker*. This *Wofong Rongker* is performed for the well-being of all the people of the villages that fall within the jurisdiction of a *Mouza* (a revenue administrative unit consisting of a number of revenue villages). Each revenue village is represented by the village headman and a number of village elders (males only) in the performance of the *Wofong Rongker*. While the *Rongker* performed for a village is only of one day's duration, the *Wofong Rongker* continues for two days" (Bordoloi, 1987 : 67). So far as the *Hacha Kekan* festival is concerned, it has been found that the festival is celebrated after the harvest. This is, in fact, a merry-making festival which is marked by community feasts, traditional dances and songs. Females are not allowed to participate. "The *Hacha Kekan* festival was not mentioned by Stack and Lyall. In that study, the traditional *Rongker* festival found a place where gods are invoked for the well-being of the people, to ward off dreadful diseases, to save the villagers from the attack of wild animals. But the *Hacha Kekan* is associated with the after harvest rejoicings. There is no fear element in it and there is no need to propitiate any god. It is not the pre-receipt prayer to god, it is rather the thanks giving ceremony where *Lakhimi,* the goddess of affluence is thanked for bestowing prosperity in the form of rice" (Bhattacharjee, 1986 : 155). In this context it may be mentioned that the Karbi Anglong autonomous Council, Diphu has declared holidays for the employess on 5th January, 15th January and 11th March for observing *Rongker*, *Hacha Kekan* and *Botor Kekur* (prayer for timely monsoon) every year.

It may be relevantly noted here that dance and music are an indispensable part of the Karbi life. The musical instruments include *pongsi* (flute), *muri* (fife), *cheng* (drum) and *kum* (one stringed fiddle) etc.

With regard to their food habit it may be said that the staple diet of the people is rice with leafy vegetables, edible roots and tubers etc. Pork, chicken and fish, particularly dry fish are their great delicacies. They use to take meals twice a day–in the morning and in the evening. Normally, the people drink black tea without milk and sugar. Ricebeer is their favourite beverage. *Eri* silk worm (*attacus ricini)* is their favourite food item.

It may not be out of place here to provide a brief introduction on their dress and ornaments. The Karbis have their traditional dress and ornaments. The women wear *mekhela* (Pini) around the waist and over it a piece of cloth called *Wamkok* is worn like a belt. Another piece of cloth (*Jiso*) is taken over the breasts. The men wear loin cloth (Rikong), shirt (*Choi)* and traditional hat (*Poho)*. At present, the pattern of dress, however, has undergone some changes, particularly among the members of the younger generation. Of course, the women have not completely given up their traditional dresses and weave necessary clothes with artistic designs in their indigenous looms (*Therang*) or in fly shuttle looms. The ornaments used by the womenfolk are generally made of silver. Gold ornaments are also used now-a-days. Bracelet (*Roi),* string of beads (*Lek),* ring (*Arnam*), ear rings (*No thengpi)* and silver tube (*Kadengchinro)* etc., are some of the ornaments used by them.

Religious Organisation

As regards religion it may be said that though Hinduism has exerted influence on the Karbis, they have still high regard for their traditional beliefs and practices. They believe in supreme God (*Arnam Kethe)*. Moreover, they believe in the existence of innumerable deities, both benevolent and malevolent and regularly worship them. The names of some of them are *Hemphu*, *Mukrang, Peng, Rasinja*, *Rit Anglong*, *Arnam Pharo*, *Chinthong Arnam*, *Chomang-ase*, *Ajo-ase* and *Theng-thon* etc. However, it is to be noted that the Karbis do not have any idol, temple or shrine. Trees and animals are not worshipped by them. People believe in witchcraft *(maja)*. When a man suffers from sickness for a prolonged period, a male diviner (*Uche)* or a female diviner (*Uchepi)* attempts to ascertain the cause of sickness by counting rice or cowry. This method is locally known as *sang-kelang-abang* (Assamese– *Mangal Soa)*. However, in this respect a which (*Lodeppi)* is considered to be more result–oriented since she has got divine power. The Karbis use charms (*pherem)* in order to cure ailments such as headache, indigestion, inflamed swelling and blood dysentery etc. Oaths and ordeals are also in practice among them. So far as human sacrifice among the people is concerned, Phangcho (1984 : 32) comments, "I am inclined to believe that the practice of human sacrifice for the satisfaction of the deities has possibly been copied from the Mon-Khmer (Austric) culture of the Khasi Syntengs. The human sacrifice was very much in vogue in *Vopong Rongker* and *Rekpi Rongker*, the two important *pujas* of the Karbis (*Deokhai Asam Buranji*). The practice of human sacrifice was widely prevalent in the *Mon-Khmer* culture of the Khasis and the Syntengs. Even the goddess Kamakhya (*Ka-meikha*, a

Khasi origin) the most esteemed and respected of all *Tantrik* and *Sakta* deities at Nilachal, Guwahati also used to receive human sacrifice from the devotees in earlier days. The Khasi *Thien*, a serpent deity often used to receive human blood which had to be provided by the keeper family. The Syntengs not only slaughtered the human being at the altar but also often held the ceremonial cannibalism (*Encyclopaedia Britannica* Vol.13,pp.361-362). Therefore, it is quite likely that the Khasi-Syntengs being more numerous and powerful, could also influence the neighbouring Karbis and probably it was followed by the Kachar is at a later date. The Karbis are so mild and meek that it is hard to accept for them to have adopted such a cult or practice as human sacrifice. It is said to be still prevalent in some of the interior places of Karbi Anglong while in the plains districts it is altogether absent".

One of the important household religious festivals of the Karbis is *Chojun* or *Swarag* which is observed at an interval of 2-3 years. The god of heaven (*Barithe)* is mainly worshipped for the welfare of the household with the help of the priest (*Kurusar)*. Moreover, *Arpi* (*Rudra), Birne* (Fire) and other minor deities are also worshipped in the festival. Pigs and fowls are sacrificed for the purpose. In order to accommodate the people in the festival small huts are constructed for females and males separately. The hut made for the females is known as *Kunturi* while that for the males is *Hamren.* Sometimes the whole village performs the festival and then it is known as *Rek Apirthat*.

However, the most important and highly expensive religious performance of the Karbis is the *Chomangkan* i.e. *Shraddha* ceremony. This is performed in order to redeem the soul of the dead. Three types of the festival are prevalent among them. These are *Kan Fla Fla*, *Langtuk* and *Harne*. Generally, the first is observed for the common people. The second is performed for the person who achieved respectable position in the society while the third is performed for the person occupying the highest social status during life-time. Since the festival involves a huge amont of expenditure, it may be organised after a long lapse of time, even after a decade of the death of a person. It may be relevantly noted here that the Karbis cremate the dead bodies in the place fixed for each clan (*Tipit)* in the cremation ground (*Thiri)*. But the dead bodies of those who commit suicide or die due to leprosy, pregnancy and attack by wild animals etc., are cremated by the riverside. They consider such unnatural death as inauspicious. In the *chomangkan*, the *Uchepi* (the woman who prepares meal for the deceased), the *Lunchepi* (female singer who requests the deceased with a pathetic tune to take meal) and the *Duhuidi* (expert drummer) play important roles. All the village people extend full co-operation and helping hands towards smooth functioning of the ceremony. The celebration may continue for 4-5 days. "Drums, pipes, shields, swords and *Jambili Athon* (a decorative wooden post) are most essential for *Chomangkan* festival. In the morning hour of the last day of *Chomangkan,* some descriptive verses called *Musera Kehir* are sung under the decorative *jambili athon*. The verses describe the legendary story of creation of human beings" (Teron, 1996).

Regarding prevalence of Christianity, it may be stated here that Christianity has gradually influenced a section of the Karbi society. The first mission centre was established in the year 1897 at Tika, 14 km away from the subdivisional H.Q. Hamren.

Traditional Administration

The traditional Karbi society is governed by a three-dimensional system of administration. At the top, there is the *Lindokpo*. At the middle, the *Habes* and at the grass root level, the *Sarthes* are the functionaries. Although the system is gradually disintegrating with the passage of time, even then the Karbi *Recho* still plays a significant role in the socioreligious life of the Karbi people, particularly inhabiting the Hamren subdivision of Karbi Anglong district.

In bygone days there were three local kings at Rongkhong, Chinthong and Amri. At present, the kings are considered as local chiefs only. Among them the highest position is occupied by the Karbi *Recho* of Rongkhong followed by the *Lindokpo* of Chinthong and the *Lindokpo* of Amri. In the Rongkhong area, there are 4 (four) *Lindokpos* selected from (i) *Ronghang* (ii) *Rongchaicho (Teron)* (iii) *Kiling* and (iv) *Rongpi sub-clans*. In the chinthong area the number of Lindokpos is 3 (three)-(i) *Chinthong* (*Hanse* sub–clan) (ii) *Nonglada* (*Rongpi* sub-clan) and (iii) *Nongpli* (*Timung Rongphar)*. Again, in the Amri area, there are 2 (two) *Lindokpos* - (i) *Du* (*Hanse* sub-clan) and (ii) *Nongkirla* (*Teron*).

The traditional capital of the Karbis is at Niz Rongkhong which is located at a distance of about 21 km from Hamren. The village is also known as Raja Gaon because of the fact that the families of the clans (four) out of which the Karbi Recho and the three *Lindokpos* of Rongkhong are chosen, reside in this village.

A *Lindokpo* is selected democratically and after his demise, the members of the respective clan select a person who is well conversant with the traditional customs. In the Rongkhong area, the Karbi *Recho* is always selected from the *Ronghang* sub-clan only.

The traditional administration is maintained by the *Lindokpo* with the help of several functionaries viz., *Dilli*, *Katharbura*, *Pator* and *Dengja* etc., who constitute the *Pinpomar* (Parliament). Moreover, the kingdom (*Hawar)* is divided into several regions which are known as *Longri. Habe* is the head of the *Longri.* He is appointed by the *Lindokpo.* Each *Longri* consists of several villages and each village is headed by a *Sarthe* who is appointed by *Habe*. It is to be noted that *Sartheship* is hereditory.

The legislative, executive and judicial powers are entrusted to the *Pinpomar.* Only when the *Pinppomar* fails to decide any case, it will then be referred to the *Lindokpo* whose *decision* will be considered as final. Again, *Arnampharo Amei* i.e. council of wise men drawn from clans and sub-clans is the supreme Appellate Authority.

With regard to this system Bhattacharjee (1986 : 58) comments, "The traditional line-up of administration is facing a challenge from the District Council. The traditional system largely depends on the willing compliance by the people and it is not backed by any enforceable coercive sanction.The Council, on the other hand, can enforce its authority because it is financially viable and also backed by proper sanction".

Village Council

It has already been mentioned above that each Karbi village is headed by a *Sarthe* (headman). Moreover, there is a village council *(Mei)*, consisting of all the adult members of the village as members *(Chakri)* and the headman as the President. In order to assist the president in the council, there are several functionaries like *Risobasa* (Assistant head-man), *Pheranke* (Informer), *Kurusar* (Priest) and *Ubebarium* (Adviser of the Bachelor's dormitory) etc. *Risobasa* holds charges of the *Mei* in the absence of the *Sarthe.* The main duty of the *Pheranke* is to inform the people when a meeting is summoned by the *Sarthe.* Moreover, he has to arrange board and lodging for the guests. The *Mei* appoints an aged and wise person to act as the adviser of the young boys of the *Jirkedam.* He is known as *Ubebarium.* He teaches the young boys not only the art of handicrafts but also about the Karbi culture. In fact, he is the linkman between *Jirkedam* and the *Mei.* Kurusar (*Deuri)* is the priest-cum-physician of the village. He performs religious duties for the welfare of the people. He also propitiates various gods with cock and wine for quick recovery of an ailing person.

The *Mei* is the primary unit of the Karbi traditional institution. It performs various development works for the benefit of the village people. It is also the trial court of the village. Disputes arising out of land ownership, adultery, theft and quarrels etc., are solved through it. Fines imposed on the guilty person generally do not exceed Rs.50.00. Cases which cannot be settled are referred to the *Habe* or *Lindokpo*. Now-a-days unsettled cases are also sent to the District Council. The *Mei* maintains law and order in the village and ensures peace amongst the people. maintenance of unity and co-operation among the people is also another objective of the *Mei.* Fixation of dates for the observation of various festivals is done through it. Moreover, in the event of death in any family of the village, the *Mei* informs the people immediately and entrusts them with various duties so that the concerned family does not face difficulties. Serious decisions like shifting of the village to a new place due to epidemic or some other reasons and distribution of *jhum* sites among the people are also taken up through the *Mei.* It is interesting to note that appeals may be made to the *Lindokpo* against the decision of the *Mei* and if necessary fines may be imposed upon the *Mei* by the highest authority.

At present, development programmes under the schemes like NREP, JRY and RLEGP etc., have been undertaken in and around the villages through the help rendered by the *Mei.* Although the schemes are not directly implemented by the *Mei,* the co-operation extended by it substantially contributes to the proper execution of the same.

Bachelor's Dormitory

The bachelor's dormitory which is known as *Terang /Farla /Jirkedam* among the Karbis is a social institution which is, in fact, an educational centre for the youths of the village to achieve manhood with dignity.

The dormitory is a pile dwelling house with thatched roof and its inside portion is decorated with artistic design. The youths of the village usually from the age of 12 years until marriage are the members and they sleep at night in the dormitory. Generally, on the eve of *Rongker* festival, the young boys of the village approach the *Sarthe* who selects the leader to carry out the activities for a period of three years. There are altogether 26 office-bearers for smooth conduct of the institution. Some of them are:

1. *Kleng sarpo*–Leader
2. *Kleng dun*–Deputy Leader
3. *Soder kethe*– Asstt. Leader
4. Soder so–Deputy Asstt. *Leader*
5. *Borlan po*–Surveyor
6. *Motan Ar*–a - Guide
7. *Motan Arvi*–Asstt. Guide
8. *Than Are*–Convenor
9. *Than Arvi*–Asstt. Convenor
10. *Chengbrup kethe*–Chief drummer
11. *Chengbrup so*–Asstt. drummer
12. *Me Apai*–Fire keeper
13. *Lang Apai*–Water keeper
14. *Kove Thok*–Collector of betel nut and leaf
15. *Phan Kri Kethe*–Distributor

Cohain (1984 : 51) provides a descriptive account on the functioning of *Jirkedam* in this manner, "In the olden days, any villager might approach the *kleng sarpo* and *kleng dun* offering them gourds of liquor for helping him in the field. *Kleng Sarpo* might accept the gourd and then would order the boys and the girls for collective work (*Jirkedam)* in the field of the villager. The boys and the girls would collect in front of the *Terang* and the *Thar-lon-po* would stand first with his measuring bamboo pole followed by the Assistant Drummer (*Chengbrup so*) on the left and the Chief Drummer on the right, followed by *Chinhak kethe*, *Chinhak so*, *Motan Ar–a*, *Motan Arvi* and others. The last boy would be the *Kleng sarpo.* Then *Banwakpi* (cloth supplier) and *Banwak so* (Assistant cloth supplier) amongst girl would follow. Other girls would follow these two. Food stuff would be collected from house to house by *Phankri kethe* and *Phankri so*. The rice was given in packet of leaves and if there was any uneatable thing in the packet the family would have to pay fine as punishment. The entrusted functionaries would carry these. In the field *Motan Arvi* and *Motan Ar–a* would take right and left positions and *Barlon po* (*Tharlon po)* would measure the land. The entire plot would be divided into two parts. In one part *Kleng dun* would be in charge, in the other *Kleng sarpo*. The *Put chekpo* would fix the index signs on the field and the *Kleng dun* would take left side while *Kleng sarpo* would take right side. All the functionaries with *Kethe* or *Po* suffix would take right side and all the functionaries with *so* suffix would take left side. The *Phankri kethe* and *Phankri so* would distribute betel nut. The other functionaries would supply specified items. After work, they would return to *Terang* systematically. In the *Terang*, *Kleng sarpo* and *Kleng dun* would take seats and take betel nut supplied by *Phankri*. The girls do not stay in the *Terang* at night. The income from the joint cultivation could be kept for 3 years and at the end of 3 years the boys and the girls would celebrate *Chojun puja* and end the *Jirkedam*. The yearly feast of the youth is called *Harlin kejun* which is attended by songs and dances".

Besides agricultural activities, the boys remain engaged in handicrafts and the girls in spinning and weaving. In marriage ceremony, *Chomangkan* (death ceremony) or any other festival held in the village, they take active part under the direction of *Kleng sarpo*. Moreover, the elderly members of the dormitory help the juniors in learning traditional dance and music in a proper manner. On the whole, the spirit of co-operation, sense of discipline and the idea of rendering social services are inculcated among the youths through the dormitory. But this important institution has practically disappeared from the Karbi society due to various forces viz., spread of modern education, impact of Christianity, practice of settled cultivation and acculturation etc. However, the reminiscence of the dormitory institution is observed in the remote areas of the district. For example, in Patikindok village, about 13 km from Ulukunchi, the members of *Jirkedam* completed the period of 3 years in February, 1991. Of course, the members did not sleep in the dormitory but they used to stay at night in their own homes. In Wanpung village under Baithalangso Police Station, *Jirkedam* is performed for 4-5 months i.e. during cultivation period only. In Dokhara Bey village under Bokajan Police Station the youths use a part of the residence of the village headman for their meetings and other occasions. It may, therefore, be assumed that the future Karbi generations will be quite at dark about the manifold activities of this institution unless the District Council authority comes forward to undertake certain positive measures for revival of the dormitory in some form or other, considering its glorious ancient past, in toto.

Youth Club

As the name signifies, it is the association of the yourths. The main function of the youth club (*Risomar*) is to perform socio-cultural activities in and around the village. An executive committee consisting of president, secretary and treasurer etc., takes the overall responsibility for smooth management of the *Risomar*. Its functions are more or less similar to the *Jirkedam* but the office-bearers are quite different. Moreover, the former is generally found in the plains portion of the district while the latter is mainly confined to the hill areas, particularly in the Hamren subdivision.

The youth club takes keen interest in traditional games and sports, dance and music etc. The youth festival which is, now-a-days, held every year with great enthusiasm in the Karbi Anglong district is perhaps the modified form of the *Risomar*. It may be noted here that some of the youth clubs have been recognised by the Karbi Anglong District Council, Diphu which has offered grants-in-aid. For example, the youth clubs of Dhentaghat, Sonapur Bey and Plong Kro under Samelangso Development Block; Phelongpi, Menmiji and Jengkailangso under Rongkhang Development Block have received financial grants from the Council authority.

Grain Bank

One of the indigenous institutions prevalent among the Karbis is the *Kerung Amei* which literally means grain bank. Its main objectives are to preserve paddy in the granary (*Apuru)* and provide assistance to the needy or poor families of the village particularly during the lean season, against interest. Thus, it plays a vital role in resisting any of the family members of the village from going to the *Mahajans* or shopkeepers for loans who charge exorbitant rate of interest. This institution not only serves as the co-operative credit society but also imparts training to the village people to extend help and co-operation towards fellow men in crisis and to save the poor families from the brink of starvation. In addition, it inspires the youths of the village to carry out social works for the welfare of the people.

Generally, three types of grain banks are functioning in the Karbi villages in the district.

Type I

All the families of the village are members of the institution and each of them has to contribute 40 kg of paddy immediately after completion of the harvest. The total amount of paddy is preserved in the granary (Apuru). When any family is in need of assistance it collects the necessary quantity of paddy on the condition that 50% interest would be paid in kind alongwith the capital after the next harvest. However, in case of widows, physically handicapped persons or patients afflicted with chronic disease etc., the interest may be exempted.

An executive committee consisting of four members is formed in order to manage the affairs relating to the grain bank. The village elders select a president and a secretary from the members. Moreover, there is one storekeeper who is in-charge of the granary. The village elders may dissolve the executive committee or remove any member if charges of malpractices are found to be true after proper verification.

Type II

The adult boys of the village carry out cultivation of paddy in a specific plot of land and the produce thus obtained is preserved in a granary. Necessary amount of paddy is given to the needy person against 50% interest while the surplus quantity is sold to the village people, normally at a discount of 10% of the ongoing market price. The entire amount is either deposited in the post office or in the rural bank. Later on, they utilise a portion of the accumulated amount to acquire land on mortgage for expansion of cultivation or for some other works like construction of village road, improvement of school building or village library etc. In this type also, an executive committee consisting of president, secretary, storekeeper and auditor takes care of the management of the grain bank.

Type III

The aged male members of the village take the responsibility of maintaining this type of greain bank. All families of the village are its members. A suitable plot of land is cultivated by them and the produce is kept in the granary. As soon as the price of paddy goes up, they sell the entire quantity of paddy and afterwards, offer the families who are in need of assistance, the required amount of money on condition that they have to repay the said amount with 100% interest. The executive committee consisting of the president, secretary, treasurer and auditor looks after the affairs of the grain bank.

Most of the grain banks located in the Karbi villages in the district are not functioning effectively except in few cases. Interestingly, there are three grain banks in Bini Hanse Gaon under Samelangso Development Block–(i) managed by women (ii) managed by men and (iii) managed by the girls only. Each bank is under the supervision of an executive committee consisting of the president, secretary and some other office-bearers. They collect 40 kg of paddy from each member and preserve the same in a godown. The needy member takes loan @ 100% interest. All the three grain banks are functioning effectively.

Status of Woman

Status of woman in the Karbi society cannot be said to be inferior to that of man. A female does not change her surname after the marriage. In fact, throughout her life, she is known by the clan in which she was born. The suffix *pi* is always used by them after their surnames to denote gender. Marriage of a girl cannot take place without proper consent of the girl. There is no purdah system among the women. In every walk of life the females are the companions of the males. Besides performing household works and taking care of the children the women work with the menfolk in clearing *jhum* lands, in collecting fire-wood from the forests, in carrying out agricultural activities and in purchasing essential commodities from the markets etc.

Of course, there are certain taboos in respect of women. A woman cannot attend the village council for any trial. They cannot partake food with the males in the community feasts. They are not allowed to participate in the *Rongker* festival.

It may, however, be relevantly noted here that during the last four decades since the creation of the district as well as the establishment of the Karbi Anglong Autonomous Council, observable positive changes have been taking place in almost all spheres of their life including 'status of woman'.

IV

THE FIELD

One of the vital factors for accelerating the socio-economic development in respect of any tribal community is attributable to the availability of infrastructural facilities and basic amenities without which proper formulation and implementation of development plans and programmes will not be possible for deriving satisfactory results. In this chapter an attempt is being made to highlight the basic infrastructural facilities available in and around the selected centres viz., Rongbong Adong, Rongnagar, Tikaklangso, Phanglangso, Mugasong, Kaipani, Kekang Adong, Thijoklagso, Langhonjar and Recho Apam. Moreover, the demographic structure of all the centres has been presented here with reasonable details. "The study of demographic data has become important in the context of national planning. No effective planning can take place unless the basic data particularly population with its socio-economic characteristics are available for a particular region" (Srivastava, 1987: xi).

Transport and Communication Facilities

It is needless to say that an improved system of transport and communication network plays an important role in uplifting the rural economy to a considerable degree. "The role of road transport in the economic life of the inhabitants of the district is of no small importance. Want of easy road communication had very often made development of the different areas a difficult task. In times of famine, relief reached too late and diseases breaking out in an epidemic form took a heavy toll of life, by the time medical aid became available to the people. Hill products, on which the villager's earnings for livelihood depend, could not be transported timely and fully and for what could be transported by head-loads and other slow means, the villagers could get only very low price.

But now with the gradually improved road system the villagers can sell their products nearer their homes and at higher price. This is also helping in creating an urge among them for increasing production" (Dutt, 1979 : 199).

So far as the field investigation in the selected centres is concerned, it has been found that the location of the centres from the nearest motorable road is not satisfactory to the desired level. In fact, out of the ten centres, five (50%) are situated at a distance of 0-4 km from the nearest motorable, four centres (40%) in the range of 5-9 km.; and one centre (10%) is as far as 25 km from the nearest motorable road. Since the people have established their villages in the interior and inaccessible hilly areas for practising shifting cultivation, they have to cover a long distance on foot to reach the nearest motorable road. However, it may be mentioned here that the motorable roads touching those centres which are, at present, devoid of roads, are under construction. As soon as the roads are completed, the people will be in a better position for their movement. But it is to be noted that if regular bus services at frequent intervals are not maintained by the private and public agencies throughout the year the people will not be able to derive maximum benefit out of this system. In this context, an example may be cited here. A State Transport bus starts from Nagaon, the headquarters of Nagaon district at about 1-30 p.m. and arrives at Ulukunchi, the headquarters of Amri Development Block at about 6-30 p.m., covering a distance of 98 km. The same bus starts from Ulukunchi the next day at 5-30 a.m., and arrives at Nagaon at 10-30 a.m. This is the only bus plying between Nagaon and Ulukunchi. As a result, the bus becomes overloaded with goods and passengers. Another bus maintained by the Karbi Anglong Autonomous Council, Diphu used to ply between Diphu and Ulukunchi via Baithalangso. But at present, this has been suspended. Finding no other alternatives, the people move to and fro in the milk vans or log carrying trucks. It is thus apparent that adequate transport facilities are essential for movement of goods and passengers of the selected centres.

With regard to the location of the centres from the nearest railway station, it may be said that not a single centre is located within easy reach of the people. The minimum distance to be covered by the people for arriving at a railway station is 15 km while the maximum distance to be covered is 91 km. In other words, only one centre (10%) is in the range of 0-20 km. from the nearest railway station. Three centres (30%) and two centres (20%) are located at a distance of 21-40 km and 41-60 km from the railway station respectively. Again, three centres (30%) are at a distance of 61-80 km while the remaining centres (10%) is in the range of 81 km. or above. The railway stations are Diphu, Hojai, Salana, Colaghat and Jagiroad. On the whole, the services rendered by the railway authorities are not easily available to the people under discussion. The approximate distance of the centres from the nearest motorable road and railway station is furnished in Table IV.1.

For the purpose of overall development of the tribal people inhabiting the Karbi Anglong district of Assam, a total number of 10 Tribal Development Blocks under the administrative control of the Karbi Anglong Autonomous Council, Diphu have been created. The present study area is confined to the jurisdiction of 7 Development Blocks viz., Lumbajong, Howraghat, Samelangso, Rongmongve, Nilip, Chinthong and Amri. The district has four Revenue Circles viz., Diphu, Phulani, Donka and Silonijan. All the surveyed centres are within these circles. Moreover, the centres fall within the jurisdictions of the Diphu, Howraghat, Bokajan and Baithalangso Police Stations. The field investigation reveals that seven centres (70%) are situated in the range of 0-30 km from the Development Block headquarters against three centres (30%) in respect of Revenue Circle as well as Police Station. In the range of 31-61 km the locations of two centres (20%), four centres (40%) and one centre (10%) are seen from the Block H.Q., Revenue Circle and Police Station respectively. Again, in the range of 62-92 km there is no centre so far as the Block H.Q. is concerned but one centre (10%) in respect of Revenue Circle and five centres (50%) in respect of Police Station are located. Moreover, one centre (10%), two centres (20%) and one centre (10%) are found at a distance of 93 km or above from the Block H.Q., Revenue Circle and Police Station respectively. On the whole, it may be said that the centres are conveniently located from the point of view of Block headquarters rather than Revenue Circle or Police Station. Table IV.2 indicates the approximate distances of the centres from the Block H.Q., Revenue Circle and Police Station.

The location of the centres from the subdivisional and district headquarters may also be mentioned here since these are the places of civil administration. There are only two centres (20%) which are located at a distance of 0-60 km from the subdivisional H.Q. and district H.Q. Seven centres (70%) lie in the range of 61-121 km from the subdivisional H.Q.,

TABLE IV.1

Distance (in Km) of the centres from the nearest Motorable Road and Railway Station

Sl. No.	Name of the Centres	Distance (in Km) from	
		Motorable Road	Railway Station
1	2	3	4
1	Rongbong Adong	8 Diphu-Guwahati	15 Diphu
2	Rongnagar	2 National highway	51 Diphu
3	Tikaklangso	3 Bakalia-Tikaklangso	62 Diphu
4	Phanglangso	3 Samelangso-Langlakso	91 Hojai
5	Mugasong	5 Dengaon-Virwar	57 Hojai
6	Kaipani	9 Nagaon-Anjokpani	25 Salana
7	Kekang Adong	0 Labonghat-Kekang Adong	32 Golaghat
8	Thijoklangso	0 Chokihola-Thijoklangso	34 Golaghat
9	Langhonjar	25 Umpanai-Nellie	80 Jagiroad
10	Recho Apam	8 Ulukunchi-Nellie	70 Jagiroad

TABLE IV.2

Distance (in Km) of the centres from the Block H.Q., Revenue Circle and Police Station

Sl. No.	*Name of the Centre*	*Distance (in km) from*		
		Development Block H.Q.	*Revenue Circle*	*Police Station*
1	*2*	*3*	*4*	*5*
1	Rongbong Adong	19 Manja, Lumbajong Block	15 Diphu	15 Diphu
2	Rongnagar	36 Manja, Lumbajong Block	21 Phulani	23 Howraghat
3	Tikaklangso	25 Howraghat, Howraghat Block	23 Phulani	25 Howraghat
4	Phanglangso	23 Samelangso, Samelangso Block	47 Phulani	63 Howraghat
5	Mugasong	45 Samelangso, Samelangso Block	33 Phulani	41 Howraghat
6	Kaipani	22 Rongmongve, Rongmongve Block	123 Phulani	147 Howraghat
7	Kekang Adong	19 Nilip, Chokihola Block	53 Silanijan	81 Bokajan
8	Thijoklangso	16 Nilip, Chokihola	55 Silanijan	83 Bokajan
9	Langhonjar	113 Chinthong, Hamren Block	98 Donkamokam	88 Baithalangso
10	Recho Apam	8 Ulukunchi, Amri Block	74 Donkamokam	64 Baithalangso

while three centres (30%) lie in the same range from the district H.Q. Again, in the range of 122-182 km one centre (10%) and two centres (20%) are found to be located from the subdivisional H.Q., and district H.Q. respectively. Moreover, there are three centres (30%) located at a distance of 183 km or above from the district H.Q. On the whole, it is apparent that the people are in a better position to visit the subdivisional H.Q., in comparison to the district H.Q. Table IV.3 shows the distance of the centres from the subdivisional H.Q., and district H.Q.

Post and Telegraph Facilities

In respect of the location of the centres from the nearest post and telegraph offices, it is seen that four centres (40%) and three centres (30%) are located at a distance of 0-5 km and 6-11 km. from the nearest post offices respectively. Again, two centres (20%) are at a distance of 12-17 km while one centre (10%) is as far as 25 km away from the nearest post office. On the contrary, one centre each is located in the ranges of 0-5 km and 6-11 km from the nearest telegraph office. Three centres (30%) are at a distance of 12-17 km while the remaining five centres (50%) are 25 km or above from the nearest telegraph office. It is, therefore, seen that the people inhabiting surveyed centres can avail of better services of the post office rather than that of the telegraph office. Table IV.4 indicates approximate distances of each centre from the nearest Post and Telegraph offices.

Medical Facilities

The people of the surveyed centres may visit the medical institutions viz., Primary Health Centre, Rural Hospital, Civil Hospital, Block Veterinary Dispensary and State Veterinary Dispensary etc., for scientific treatment of the diseases which may inflict upon the people or their livestock. However, the distance to be covered by them for visiting the nearest health services establishments varies from centre to centre. The present investigation reveals that out of ten centres, 7 (70%) are located at a distance of 0-20 km from the nearest PHC/Rural Hospital. But there are 1, 4 and 3 centres that are located in the same range of distance from the nearest Civil Hospital, Block Veterinary Dispensary and State Veterinary Dispensary respectively. Again, it is seen that there are 3, 2, 5 and 3 centres that are located at a distance of 21-41 km from the nearest PHC/ Rural Hospital, Civil Hospital, Block Veterinary Dispensary and State Veterinary Dispensary respectively. This reveals that all the ten centres

TABLE IV.3

Distance (in km) of the centres from the subdivisional H.Q. and District H.Q.

Sl. No.	*Name of the Centre*	*Distance (in km) from*	
		Subdivisional H.Q.	*District H.Q.*
1	*2*	*3*	*4*
1	Rongbong Adong	15 Diphu	15 Diphu
2	Rongnagar	51 Diphu	51 Diphu
3	Tikaklangso	63 Diphu	63 Diphu
4	Phanglangso	115 Diphu	115 Diphu
5	Mugasong	105 Diphu	105 Diphu
6	Kaipani	155 Bokajan	220 Diphu
7	Kekang Adong	81 Bokajan	151 Diphu
8	Thijoklangso	83 Bokajan	153 Diphu
9	Langhonjar	113 Hamren	220 Diphu
10	Recho Apam	89 Hamren	196 Diphu

TABLE IV.4

Distance (in km) of the centres from the nearest Post & Telegraph Office

Sl. No.	*Name of the Centre*	*Distance (in km) from*	
		Post Office	*Telegraph Office*
1	*2*	*3*	*4*
1	Rongbong Adong	15 Diphu	15 Diphu
2	Rongnagar	4 Bakalia	4 Bakalia
3	Tikaklangso	7 Bakalia	7 Bakalia
4	Phanglangso	3 Langlakso	39 Langhing
5	Mugasong	17 Dengaon	23 Dokmoka
6	Kaipani	9 Anjokpani	25 Salana
7	Kekang Adong	2 Deithor	14 Numaligarh
8	Thijoklangso	4 Deithor	16 Numaligarh
9	Langhonjar	25 Umpanai	66 Nellie
10	Recho Apam	8 Ulukunchi	56 Nellie

TABLE IV.5

Distance (in km) of the centres from the nearest Medical Institutions

Sl. No.	*Name of the Centres*	*Distance (in km) from*			
		Primary Health Centre/Rural Hospital	*Cioil Hospital*	*Block Vety. Disp.*	*State Vety. Disp.*
1	*2*	*3*	*4*	*5*	*6*
1	Rongbong Adong	19 Manja PHC	15 Diphu	19 Manja	15 Diphu
2	Rongnagar	5 Bakalia R.H.	51 Diphu	23 Howraghat	5 Bakalia
3	Tikaklangso	8 Bakalia R.H.	62 Diphu	25 Howraghat	7 Bakalia
4	Phanglangso	31 Dentaghat R.H.	139 Diphu	23 Samelangso	47 Phulani
5	Mugasong	17 Dengaon PHC	105 Diphu	45 Samelangso	33 Phulani
6	Kaipani	28 Simana PHC	65 Nagaon	22 Rongmongve	65 Nagaon
7	Kekang Adong	2 Deithor PHC	32 Golaghat	19 Chokihola	32 Golaghat
8	Thijoklangso	4 Deithor PHC	34 Golaghat	16 Chokihola	34 Golaghat
9	Langhonjar	25 Umpanai PHC	115 Nagaon	32 Ulukunchi	66 Nellie
10	Recho Apam	11 Putsari PHC	106 Nagaon	8 Ulukunchi	56 Nellie

are situated within the broad range of 0-41 km. from the nearest PHC/Rural Hospital. In the range of 42-62 km there are two centres (20%) from the Civil Hospital, one centre (10%) from the Block Veterinary Dispensary and two centres (20%) from the State Veterinary Dispensary. Again, one centre (10%) is located at a distance of 63-83 km from the nearest Civil Hospital and two centres (20%) are located in the same range of distance from the State Veterinary Dispensary. Moreover, four centres (40%) lie at a distance of more than 100 km from the nearest Civil Hospital. Thus, it seems, the locations of Primary Health Centre/Rural Hospital and Block Veterinary Dispensary are within a relatively more convenient distance from the people rather than that of the Civil Hospital or State Veterinary Dispensary. However, it is to be noted that a section of the people inhabiting the centres are in the habit of using indigenous drugs made of wild herbs and roots, offering worship/sacrifice to the gods and goddesses alongwith various *mantras* being chanted by the *Ojha* for treatment of diseases. They proceed to the medical centres only when they do not succeed in getting the desired results from the above means. Moreover, it may not be out of place to mention here that some of the medical institutions lack in adequate staff, scientific equipments and requisite medicines for proper treatment. As a consequence, the people have to proceed to the district headquarters viz., Diphu, Nagaon and Golaghat etc., for treatment of certain diseases. The exercise involves substantial amount of money, time and energy. Table IV.5 shows the distances of the centres from the nearest medical institutions.

Educational Facilities

All the centres under discussion have been provided with Lower Primary Schools by the Karbi Anglong Autonomous Council, Diphu. In respect of the location of the centres in relation to the nearest Middle and High Schools it is seen that out of the ten centres, 5 (50%) and 3 (30%) are located at a distance of 0-4 km from the nearest Middle and High School respectively. Again, in the range of 5-9 km there are three centres (30%) from the Middle School against four centres (40%) from the nearest High School. Two centres (20%) and one centre (10%) are situated at a distance of 10-14 km from the nearest Middle and High School respectively. Two centres (20%) are located beyond 15 km. from the nearest High School. So far as the Higher Secondary or College education is concerned, it is seen that out of the ten centres, 6 (60%) and 2 (20%) are situated at a distance of 0-30 km and 31-61 km from the nearest H.S.S. and College respectively.

TABLE IV.6

Distance (in km) of the centres from the nearest Educational Institutions

Sl. No.	Name of the Centres	Distance (in km) from			
		Lower Primary School	Middle School	High School	H.S.S./ College
1	2	3	4	5	6
1	Rongbong Adong	Within Village	12 Birla	12 Birla	15 Diphu
2	Rongnagar	Within Village	5 Bakalia	5 Bakalia	5 Bakalia
3	Tikaklangso	Within Village	Within Village	7 Bakalia	7 Bakalia
4	Phanglangso	Within Village	3 Langlakso	3 Langlakso	45 Dokmoka
5	Mugasong	Within Village	12 Virwar	17 Dengaon	23 Dokmoka
6	Kaipani	Within Village	7 Blijuri	9 Anjokpani	35 Kaliabor
7	Kekang Adong	Within Village	Within Village	2 Deithor	17 Marangi
8	Thijoklangso	Within Village	3 Kang Adong	4 Deithor	19 Marangi
9	Langhonjar	Within Village	6 Umlapher	25 Umpanai	80 Jagiroad
10	Recho Apam	Within Village	1 Achomkimi	8 Ulukunchi	70 Jagiroad

Again two centres (20%) are located in the range of 62-92 km from the nearest H.S.S./College. The approximate distances of the centres from the nearest educational institutions have been furnished in Table IV.6.

The total number of students from the centres attending the Lower Primary Schools, during the time of investigation has been found to be 330 out of which male and female students are 194 (58.79% and 136 (41.21%) respectively. On the other hand, the total number of students attending Middle Schools from the centres is 120, the male and female students being 84 (70%) and 36 (30%) respectively. The total number of students attending High Schools from the centres is 112 out of which the number of males is 78 (69.64%) and that of the females is 34 (30.36%). Thus, the number of students attending Middle and High Schools shows a decreasing trend after primary level of education. Moreover, the attendance of the females in the educational institutions is found to be less in comparison to that of the males. Perhaps the indifference of the guardians towards female education is one of the responsible factors. The study further reveals that the number of students reading in Higher Secondary or College level is 7 only, the male and female students being 5 and 2 respectively. This clearly indicates that the higher education is yet to make a proper in-road among the people of the surveyed centres. Table IV.7 shows the number of students in the educational institutions from the centres.

In this context, the literacy position among the population in the selected centres may also be referred to. The total population in the centres is 2,865 out of which the number of literates is 905 (31.59%). The percentage of male literacy is 40.30 while that of the female literacy is 22.23. According to 1991 Census the percentage of literacy in the district of Karbi Anglong is 35.88, the percentages of male and female literacy being 44.15 and 26.76 respectively. Thus, the rate of literacy in the surveyed centres is comparatively less than that of the district as a whole. On the other hand, the number of illiterates in the centres is 1,960, the male and female illiterates being 886 and 1074 respectively. In terms of percentage it is found that the total illiterates constitute 68.41 of the total population. The percentages of male and female illiterates are 59.70 and 77.77 respectively. On the whole, the centres need relatively more attention in terms of infrastructural facilities as well as motivation to enable the people to improve their educational scenario. Table IV.8 indicates the distribution of the population according to the level of education.

TABLE IV.7

Number of students reading in the educational institutions from the centres

Sl. No.	Name of the Centres	Number of students							
		L.P. Standard		M.E. Standard		H.E. Standard		H.S.S./ College	
		M	F	M	F	M	F	M	F
1	2	3	4	5	6	7	8	9	10
1	Rongbong Adong	16	5	6	2	3	-	-	-
2	Rongnagar	39	28	20	8	13	3	2	-
3	Tikaklangso	26	29	5	3	4	-	-	-
4	Phanglangso	16	13	10	1	1	3	-	-
5	Mugasong	18	9	3	1	-	-	-	-
6	Kaipani	21	14	9	-	3	1	-	-
7	Kekang Adong	10	9	6	10	12	8	1	-
8	Thijoklangso	8	5	10	6	37	18	2	2
9	Langhonjar	21	11	9	3	3	-	-	-
10	Recho Apam	19	13	6	2	2	-	-	-
	Total	194	136	84	36	78	34	5	2

Marketing Facilities

"The market occupies a pivotal role in the economic and social life of the people. It is the place where men and women from different walks of life gather, and sometimes for economic reasons–are often compelled to rise above narrow considerations of caste, creed, religion and language. A dent, though temporary, is made on the otherwise conservative mental frame work and this provides an excellent opportunity for positive socio-economic activities. The market can be used very effectively for exchanging social ideas and also for studying the economy of the people" (Biswas, 1984 : 203).

The daily/weekly markets where the people of the centres can participate are located at considerable distances, and are not easily accessible to them. Only one centre (10%) lies at a distance of 0-5 km from the nearest daily and weekly market. Two centres (20%) and six centres (60%) are in the range of 6-11 km from the daily and weekly markets respectively. Again, three centres (30%) are at a distance of 12-17 km from the daily market while two centres (20%) are located in the same range from the nearest weekly market. Moreover, one centre (10%) is 18 km away from the nearest daily/weekly market. The people inhabiting the centres proceed to the nearest market in order to purchase their essential commodities viz., cloth, salt, sugar, kerosene, tea, rice, atta, bidi and tobacco etc. On the other hand, they sell their produces like rice, maize, sesame, ginger, chilli and other vegetables in the market. Sometimes pork and poultry are also sold by them in the nearest market. Table IV.9 shows the nearest market place with its type and distance from each centres.

Lamps and Banks

So far as the location of the Large Area Multipurpose Co-operative Societies (LAMPS) is concerned, it is seen that three centres (30%) and two centres (20%) are situated at a distance of 0-5 km and 6-11 km respectively from the LAMPS. The remaining five centres (50%) are, however, located in the broad range of 12-32 km from the nearest LAMPS. It is, therefore, seen that the people of the centres have to face difficulties in getting economic benefits out of the LAMPS. As a matter of fact, the people do not seem to be much conscious about the facilities provided by the co–operative societies.

With the establishment of the Langpi Dehangi Rural Bank in 1982 the banking facilities in Karbi Anglong district have geared up to a

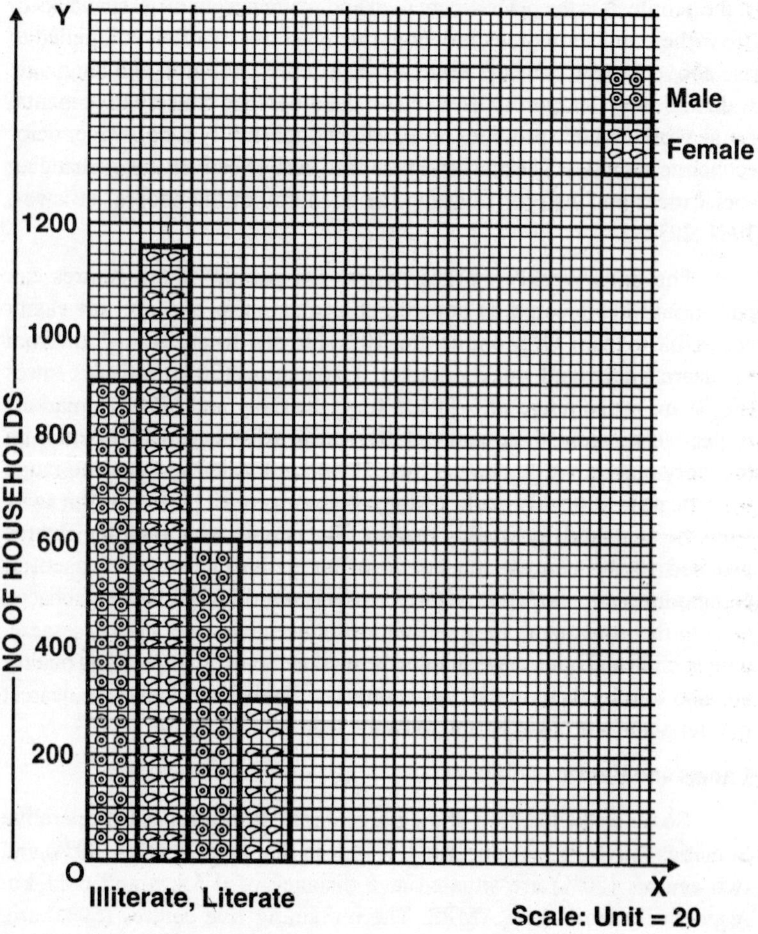

Fig. 1. Histogram showing the Position of Literates and Illiterates by Sex.

TABLE IV.8

Distribution of the population according to the level of education

Sl. No.	Name of the Centre	Level of Education									
		L.P. Standard		M.E. Standard		H.E. Standard		H.S.L.C. & Above		Illiterates	
		M	F	M	F	M	F	M	F	M	F
1	2	3	4	5	6	7	8	9	10	1!	1
1	Rongbong Adong	17	5	8	2	3	-	-	-	95	116
2	Rongnagar	45	35	35	18	33	11	5	1	113	146
3	Tikaklangso	34	31	17	3	5	-	-	-	94	122
4	Phanglangso	28	17	24	3	3	3	-	-	101	117
5	Mugasong	24	16	6	3	1	1	-	-	29	26
6	Kaipani	40	15	21	7	9	3	-	-	97	133
7	Kekang Adong	17	17	19	18	33	17	5	2	50	53
8	Thijoklangso	11	6	21	7	47	22	2	2	59	63
9	Langhonjar	25	15	12	5	6	-	-	-	153	193
10	Recho Apam	21	16	13	5	8	1	-	-	95	105
	Total	262	173	176	71	148	58	12	5	886	1074

TABLE IV.9

Number of nearest market place with its type and distance from the centres

Sl. No.	*Name of the Centre*	*Name of the Market*	*Type*	*Distance from the Centre (in km)*
1	*2*	*3*	*4*	*5*
1	Rongbong Adong	Diphu	Daily Weekly (Wed.)	15
2	Rongnagar	Bakalia	Daily Weekly (Tues.)	5
3	Tikaklangso	Bakalia	Daily Weekly (Tues.)	7
4	Phanglangso	Samelangso	Daily Weekly (Thurs.)	23
5	Mugasong	Dengaon	Daily Weekly (Thurs.)	17
6	Kaipani	Balijuri	Weekly (Wed.)	9
7	Kekang Adong	Namaligarh Bihara	Daily Weekly (Sun.)	10 7
8	Thijoklangso	Numaligarh Bihara	Daily Weekly (Sun.)	12 9
9	Langhonjar	Umlaphar	Weekly (Sat.)	6
10	Recho Apam	Birsingki	Weekly (Fri.)	10

TABLE IV.10
Distance (in km.) of the centres from the nearest LAMPS and Banks

Sl. No.	*Name of the Centres*	*Distance (in km) from* *Lamps*	*Banks*
1	*2*	*3*	*4*
1	Rongbong Adong	19 Manja	15 Diphu
2	Rongnagar	5 Bakalia	5 Bakalia
3	Tikaklangso	7 Bakalia	7 Bakalia
4	Phanglangso	31 Dentaghat	23 Samelangso
5	Mugasong	17 Dengaon	17 Dengaon
6	Kaipani	9 Anjokpani	25 Salana
7	Kekang Adong	2 Deithor	2 Deithor
8	Thijoklangso	4 Deithor	4 Deithor
9	Langhonjar	25 Umpanai	32 Ulukunchi
10	Recho Apam	15 Umpanai	8 Ulukunchi

considerable extent. There are about 34 branches of this rural bank all over the district. Moreover, the branches of SBI, CBI, UBI, UCO, Bank of Baroda, Union Bank and Assam Co-operative Apex Bank located in different parts of the district have been catering the needs of the people. However, the investigation reveals that the surveyed centres are not conveniently located to get easy access to the nearest Bank. Three centres (30%) are situated at a distance of 0-5 km while two centres (20%) are found at a distance of 6-11 km from the nearest Bank. The location of the remaining five centres (50%) is in the broad range of 12–32 km. In this context, it may be mentioned here that the habit of savings among the people of the surveyed centres appears to be lacking. Moreover, the people do not like to go to the Banks for necessary help due to the complicated procedures involved in the same. Table IV.10 shows the distance of the centres from the nearest LAMPS and Banks.

Sources of Drinking Water

Drinking water facilities available to the people of the centres during the present investigation do not seem to be very satisfactory. Out of the ten centres, tap water is available in one centre only. Similarly, tubewells are installed in one centre. Generally the people take water from the ponds, wells, rivers and natural springs etc. Which they take by and large without any prior purificatory treatment. This may be one of the possible factors that contribute towards the observed higher incidence of water-borne diseases among them. There are altogether 32 ponds, 34 wells, 8 rivers and 3 natural springs in the micro-field under investigation. Details are furnished in Table IV.11.

Electricity

Out of the ten centres, electricity is available in three centres (30%) only. These are Rongnagar, Kekang Adong and Thijoklangso. The people have been found to use electricity for household consumption and not for agricultural purpose.

Demographic Structure

It has already been mentioned that all the ten centres under study are homogenously inhabited by the Karbis. The total households in the centres are 533. The distribution of the households according to size in different centres is furnished in Table IV.12. The table reveals that the highest households numbering 321 (60.23%) are found in the category of

TABLE IV.11

Sources of drinking water in the centres

Sl. No.	*Name of the Centres*	*Sources of water*					
		Pond	*Well*	*River*	*Spring*	*Tube-well*	*Tap water*
1	*2*	*3*	*4*	*5*	*6*	*7*	*8*
1	Rongbong Adong	4	3	1	-	-	-
2	Rongnagar	12	8	1	-	7	-
3	Tikaklangso	-	2	1	-	-	-
4	Phanglangso	2	3	-	1	-	-
5	Mugasong	-	3	1	-	-	-
6	Kaipani	4	3	-	2	-	-
7	Kekang Adong	4	3	1	-	-	PHE
8	Thijoklangso	1	4	1	-	-	-
9	Langhonjar	3	2	1	-	-	-
10	Recho Apam	2	3	1	-	-	-
	Total	32	34	8	3	7	

'4-6' members (medium) while the lowest households numbering 22 (4.12%) are found in the category of '10 & above' (very large). Moreover, there are 85 (15.95%) and 105 households (19.7%) in the categories '3 or less' members (small) and '7-9' members (large) respectively. Thus, the modal size of a household ranges from 4 to 6 members and the modal frequency is 321. The average size of a household however, is 5.38.

While dealing with the distribution of the centres by the size of population, it is seen that out of the ten centres, one (10%) falls within the category 'below 200'. As many as seven centres (70%) fall within the category of '200-400' while two centres (20%) are within the category of '401 and above'. Table IV.13 shows the distribution of the centres by the size of population.

With regards to the distribution of the population according to age group it may be said that the highest population numbering 1,206 (42.09%) is found in the age group '0-15' yrs. while the lowest population numbering 84 (2.93%) is found in the age group '61 yrs. and above'. Again, in the age group of '16-30' yrs the population is 762 which accounts for 26.60% of the total population. In the age group of '31-45' yrs. the number of population is worked out to be 545 (19.02%) against 268 (9.35%) in the age group of '46.60' yrs. This indicates that the percentages of population to the total population are decreasing from the age group '0-15' yrs. upwards. Table IV.14 shows the distribution of population according to age group in the centres. "The age structure of population is one of the most important demographic factors determining the level of socio-economic development in different regions. For an economy to be efficient, there must be a relatively high percentage of persons in the active age group and low percentage of persons in the dependent age groups" (Das, 1984 : 33). In order to find out the total working force in the centres, the two age groups '0-15' yrs and '61 yrs & above' covering altogether 1,290 persons may be considered as dependent age group while the remaining age groups '16-30' yrs, '31-45' yrs and '46-60' yrs covering 1,575 persons may be considered as active age group. The percentages of population in the active and dependent age groups are found to be 54.97 and 45.03 respectively.

With regard to the marital status of the people under discussion, it will be seen from Table IV.15 that out of the total population of 2,865, 1,068 persons (37.28%) are married 1,690 (58.99%) unmarried and 107 individuals

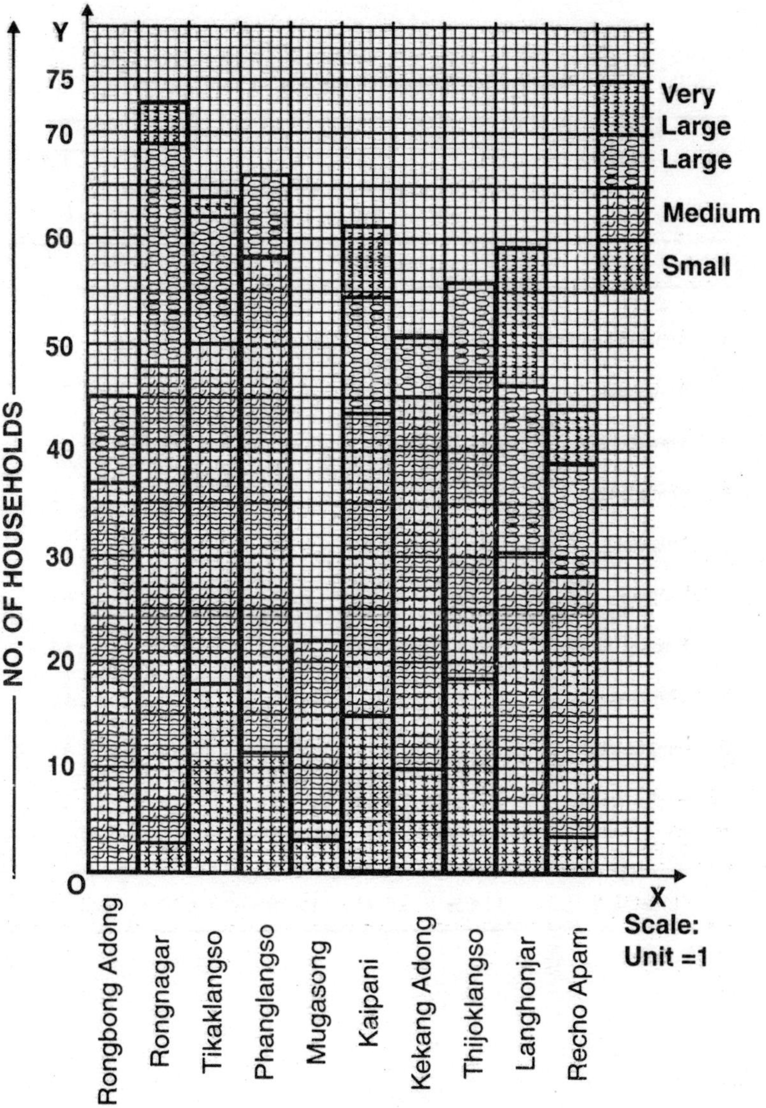

Fig. 2. Sub-divided Bar Diagram showing the Distribution of Household Size in the Centres

TABLE IV.12

Distribution of household size in the centres

Sl. No.	*Name of the Centre*	*Size of households with members*				
		Small 3 or less	*Medium 4-6*	*Large 7-9*	*Very large 10 & above*	*Total house holds*
1	*2*	*3*	*4*	*5*	*6*	*7*
1	Rongbong Adong	-	38	7	-	45
2	Rongnagar	3	44	22	3	72
3	Tikaklangso	17	33	12	1	63
4	Phanglangso	11	47	7	-	65
5	Mugasong	3	20	-	-	23
6	Kaipani	14	28	14	5	61
7	Kekang Adong	9	36	5	-	50
8	Thijoklangso	16	31	7	-	54
9	Langhonjar	7	20	19	10	56
10	Recho Apam	5	24	12	3	44
	Total	85	321	105	22	533
	Percentage	15.95	60.23	19.70	4.12	100.00

TABLE IV-13

Distribution of the centres by size of population

Sl. No.	*Name of the Centre*	*Total Population*			*Remarks, if any*
		below 200	*200-400*	*401 & above*	
1	*2*	*3*	*4*	*5*	*6*
1	Rongbong Adong		246		Total population (10 centres) = 2,865
2	Rongnagar			442	
3	Tikaklangso		306		
4	Phanglangso		296		
5	Mugasong	106			
6	Kaipani		325		
7	Kekang Adong		231		
8	Thijoklangso		240		
9	Langhonjar			409	
10	Recho Apam		264		

(3.73%) are widowed. The table also reveals that among the unmarried persons the number of males (917) is higher than that of the females (773). As a matter of fact, 61.79% of the males are unmarried against 55.97% of the females. The percentage of married males (35.98%) is relatively low than that of the married females (38.67%). It is also seen that marriage of either a male or a female has not taken place 16 years of age. The number of widows with a total of 74 is substantially higher than that of the widowers with a total of 33 (2.22%) only. This probably reflects the fact that the life-span of a woman is by and large relatively more than that of a man. This observation however, does not ignore the reality that a husband is usually older than the wife.

Sex Ratio

In an agrarian economy sex ratio is a vital factor to be taken into consideration because of the fact that the tribal womenfolk play an important role in the economic activities. It is generally believed that they are more laborious than the menfolk. Besides household works, they remain engaged in agricultural activities practically throughout the year and thus they contribute a lot towards augmentation of their economic conditions.

> "Normally the sex ratio in a population should be around 1000, the deviance of sex ratio is a social fact that requires a sociological answer. Biologically, about 105 male babies are born for 100 female babies. And since the biological chance of dying at each stage is higher for males..., one expects that the total population will contain more or less equal number of persons of both sexes" (Sharma, 1989 : 74).

The present investigation reveals that the sex ratio of the total population is 1000 : 930. According to 1991 Census the sex ratio in the district of Karbi Anglong is 1000 : 907. Thus, the number of females per 1000 males in the surveyed centres is slightly higher than that of the district. It may also be noted here that in two centres the female population exceeds the male population while in one centre the number of male and female population is equal. The sex ratio is highest in Langhonjar (1000 : 1086) and lowest in Thijoklangso (1000 : 714). Table IV.16 displays the sex ratio in the studied centres.

On the whole, in socio-demographic characteristics as well as in infrastructural amenities the centres under investigation, by and large, reflect the overall characteristics of all the centres of the district.

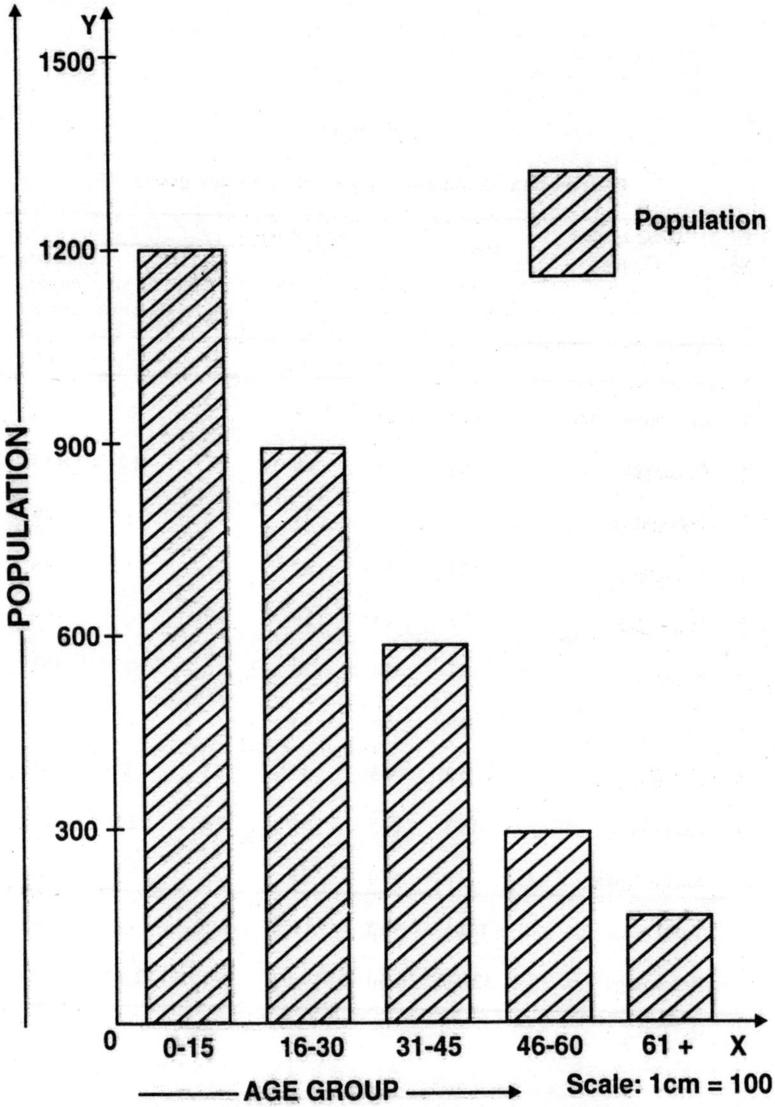

Fig. 3. Bar diagram showing the Distribution of Population according to Age group

TABLE IV.14

Distribution of population according to age group

Sl. No.	Name of the Centre	Age group					
		0-15 Yrs.	16-30 Yrs.	31-45 Yrs.	46-60 Yrs.	61 yrs & above	Total population
1	2	3	4	5	6	7	8
1	Rongbong Adong	120	45	55	21	5	246
2	Rongnagar	195	141	69	25	12	442
3	Tikaklangso	146	57	71	27	5	306
4	Phanglangso	124	65	82	24	1	296
5	Mugasong	38	25	33	10	–	106
6	Kaipani	141	74	73	30	7	325
7	Kekang Adong	69	85	41	25	11	231
8	Thijoklangso	60	85	37	53	5	240
9	Langhonjar	195	115	50	28	21	409
10	Recho Apam	118	70	34	25	17	264
	Total	1206	762	545	268	84	2865
	Percentage	42.10	26.60	19.02	9.35	2.93	100.00

TABLE IV.15

Distribution of the marital status of population of the centres by age and sex

Sl. No.	Name of the Centre	Age group	Marital Status						Total population		
			Unmarried		Married		Widow/Widower				
			M	F	M	F	M	F	M	F	Total
1	2	3	4	5	6	7	8	9	10	11	12
1	Rongbong Adong	0 - 15	58	62	-	-	-	-	58	62	120
		16 - 30	17	14	2	12	-	-	19	26	45
		31 - 45	1	-	28	26	-	-	29	26	55
		46 - 60	-	-	13	8	-	-	13	8	21
		61 +	-	-	4	1	-	-	4	1	5
2	Rongnagar	0 - 15	107	88	-	-	-	-	107	88	195
		16 - 30	47	39	22	33	-	-	69	72	141
		31 - 45	-	-	38	30	-	1	38	31	69
		46 - 60	-	-	8	7	1	9	9	16	25
		61 +	-	-	5	3	3	1	8	4	12

continued ....

TABLE IV-15

1	2	3	4	5	6	7	8	9	10	11	12
		0 - 15	66	80	-	-	-	-	66	80	146
		16 - 30	22	7	10	18	-	-	32	25	57
3	Tikaklangso	31 - 45	3	-	37	30	-	1	40	31	71
		46 - 60	-	-	11	10	-	6	11	16	27
		61 +	-	-	1	1	-	3	1	4	5
		0 - 15	63	61	-	-	-	-	63	61	124
		16 - 30	27	11	6	21	-	-	33	32	65
4	Phanglangso	31 - 45	-	-	42	38	-	2	42	40	82
		46 - 60	-	-	17	7	-	-	17	7	24
		61 +	-	-	1	-	-	-	1	-	1
		0 - 15	22	16	-	-	-	-	22	16	38
		16 - 30	13	8	-	4	-	-	13	12	25
5	Mugasong	31 - 45	2	-	15	15	1	-	18	15	33
		46 - 60	-	-	6	2	1	1	7	3	10
		61 +	-	-	-	-	-	-	-	-	-

continued ....

1	2	3	4	5	6	7	8	9	10	11	12
		0 - 15	70	71	-	-	-	-	70	71	141
		16 - 30	25	14	15	20	-	-	40	34	74
6	Kaipani	31 - 45	3	-	35	33	1	1	39	34	73
		46 - 60	-	-	13	10	3	4	16	14	30
		61 +	-	-	-	-	2	5	2	5	7
		0 - 15	34	35	-	-	-	-	34	35	69
		16 - 30	29	22	14	20	-	-	43	42	85
7	Kekang Adong	31 - 45	11	-	12	16	-	2	23	18	41
		46 - 60	-	-	12	7	3	3	15	10	25
		61 +	-	-	6	1	3	1	9	2	11
		0 - 15	32	28	-	-	-	-	32	28	60
		16 - 30	54	21	2	8	-	-	56	29	85
8	Thijoklangso	31 - 45	1	1	7	28	-	-	8	29	37
		46 - 60	-	-	34	10	5	4	39	14	53
		61 +	-	-	3	-	2	-	5	-	5

continued..........

1	2	3	4	5	6	7	8	9	10	11	12
		0 - 15	94	101	-	-	-	-	94	101	195
		16 - 30	30	26	20	38	1	-	51	64	115
9	Langhonjar	·31 - 45	-	-	26	22	-	2	26	24	50
		46 - 60	-	-	15	7	-	6	15	13	28
		61 +	-	-	8	2	2	9	10	11	21
		0 - 15	61	57	-	-	-	-	61	57	118
		16 - 30	23	11	13	23	-	-	36	34	70
10	Recho Apam	31 - 45	2	-	17	13	-	2	19	15	34
		46 - 60	-	-	11	10	1	3	12	13	25
		61 +	-	-	5	-	4	8	9	8	17
	Sub Total		917	773	534	534	33	74	1484	1381	
	Percentage (Male & Female)		61.79	55.97	35-98	38.67	2.22	5.36	100	100	
	Total		1690		1068		107		2865		2865
	Percentage (M +F)		58.99		37.28		3.73		100.00		100.00

TABLE IV.16

Sex Ratio in the Centres

Sl. No.	*Name of the Centres*	*Male*	*Female*	*Female per 1000 males*
1	*2*	*3*	*4*	*5*
1	Rongbong Adong	123	123	1000
2	Rongnagar	231	211	913
3	Tikaklangso	150	156	1040
4	Phanglangso	156	140	897
5	Mugasong	60	46	766
6	Kaipani	167	158	946
7	Kekang Adong	124	107	862
8	Thijoklangso	140	100	714
9	Langhonjar	196	213	1086
10	Recho Apam	137	127	927
	Total	1484	1381	930

V

ECONOMIC PROFILE OF THE PEOPLE AND THE PROGRAMME

Agriculture is the mainstay of the people inhabiting the district of Karbi Anglong which is one of the most backward districts of Assam. Nearly 90 per cent of the total population of this district depend upon agriculture including shifting cultivation as the main source of livelihood. This chapter attempts to analyse the occupational structure, land-holding pattern and extent of income and expenditure among the people inhabiting the IJDP centres under study. Moreover, the welfare schemes implemented under the IJDP in the studied centres have also been taken into account in this chapter.

Occupational Structure

With a view to presenting the occupational structure of the households, the occupations pursued by the different members of the family have conveniently been classified as 'primary' and 'secondary' occupations. "The source which contributes the largest single share to the total family income is considered as the primary occupation of the household. Other associated source of income, if any, are taken as secondary occupations of the households" (Saikia, 1968 : 26). Data generated from the field reveal that out of the total households of 533, the number of households practising cultivation as the primary occupation is 520, the percentage being 97.56. Only ten-households (1.88%) have accepted service as primary occupation. On the other hand, the number of households practising contract or business as primary occupation is a meagre 3 (0.56%). It is, thus, apparent that agriculture plays a pivotal role in the economy of the people under study. So far as the secondary occupation is concerned, it is seen that out of 533 households, 13 (2.44%) practise cultivation as secondary occupation. Six (1.13%) and seven households (1.31%) have accepted service and contract/business as secondary occupation respectively. But it is to be notes that 47 households (8.82%) have adopted daily wage as secondary occupation for their sustenance. Table V.1 shows the distribution of Primary and Secondary occupations in the selected centres.

The total population in all the ten centres has been classified into earners, earning dependents and non-earning dependents in order to know the numerical position as well as proportion of workers and non-workers in the centres. The category 'earners' includes those persons who contribute a significant amount of income towards maintenance of the households. In fact, only one person, preferably the head of the household or the person whose share of income is proportionately more is taken into account in this category. Again, the category 'earning dependents' includes all the members of the households in the age group "15-65' years. On the contrary, those who are below 15 years and above 65 years of age are included in the category 'non-earning dependents'. Both earners and earning dependents are included in the group 'workers' while non-earning dependents are included in the group 'non-workers'. It has been found that out of the total population of 2,865, the number of earners is 533 which constitutes 18.60% of the total population. The number of earning dependents has been found to be 1,198, the percentage being 41.82. Again, the number of non-earning dependents is 1,134 (39.58%). Thus, it seems that the number of earners is proportionately less. It may however, be relevantly noted here that the females and other adult members including students contribute significantly towards the maintenance of the families among the Karbis. As a matter of fact, this is a common feature in a tribal society. As a result, the earners and earning dependents together constitute the potential working force. The total number of workers is found to be 1,731, the percentage being 60.42. On the other hand, the non-workers or non-earning dependents numbering 1,134 constitute 39.58% of the total population. Table V.2 reflects the position of workers and non-workers in the centres.

Land-Holding Pattern

It is indeed a difficult task to discuss the land-holding pattern

TABLE V.1

Distribution of primary and secondary occupations in the studied centres

Sl. No.	*Name of the Centre*	*No. of house-holds*	*Primary occupation*			*Secondary Occupation*			
			Culti-vation	*Primary Occupation Service*	*Contract/ Business*	*Culti-vation*	*Service*	*Contract/ Business*	*Daily labour*
1	*2*	*3*	*4*	*5*	*6*	*7*	*8*	*9*	*10*
1	Rongbong Adong	45	44	1	-	1	-	-	3
2	Rongnagar	72	68	4	-	4	3	5	6
3	Tikaklangso	63	63	-	-	-	-	-	5
4	Phanglangso	65	64	1	-	1	-	-	7
5	Mugasong	23	22	1	-	1	-	-	4
6	Kaipani	61	61	-	-	-	1	-	3
7	Kekang Adong	50	44	3	3	6	1	1	5
8	Thijoklangso	54	54	-	-	-	1	1	6
9	Langhonjar	56	56	-	-	-	-	-	5
10	Recho Apam	44	44	-	-	-	-	-	3
	Total	533	520	10	3	13	6	7	47
	Percentage		97.56	1.88	0.56	2.44	1.13	1.31	8.82

TABLE V.2

Distribution of workers and non-workers in the studied centres

Sl. No.	*Name of the Centre*	*Banner*	*Earning Dependent*	*Non-earning Dependent*	*Total population*
1	*2*	*3*	*4*	*5*	6
1	Rongbong Adong	45	94	107	246
2	Rongnagar	72	185	185	442
3	Tikaklangso	63	102	141	306
4	Phanglangso	65	124	107	296
5	Mugasong	23	43	40	106
6	Kaipani	61	126	138	325
7	Kekang Adong	50	117	64	231
8	Thijoklangso	54	143	43	240
9	Langhonjar	56	164	189	409
10	Recho Apam	44	100	120	264
	Total	533	1198	1134	286
	Percentage	18.60	41.82	39.58	100.00

prevalent not only in the IJDP centres but also in the two autonomous hill districts of Assam as a whole. This is mainly because the people generally practise the traditional method of shifting cultivation. The quantity of land possessed by a household may vary from year to year depending upon the area brought under cultivation in a particular year. Moreover, lack of land records from the cadastral survey also stands in the way of presenting the actual position.

Chowdhury (1992 : 12) observes, "Cadastral survey and systematic preparation and maintenance of land records etc., were started in the plains districts of undivided Assam in 1883 and the process is continuing till date. But this was not the case in respect of the Hill districts. Till 1975-76, except improvised survey by crude methods of the indigenous survey instruments as required from time to time as per possessions of land by individual families, group of persons, organisations and Government and public purposes, scientific and systematic survey work and preparation of land records remained practically absent in both the districts of Karbi Anglong and N.C.Hills. There was no proper classification and assessment of land as per use. For the first time in the history of these districts, in 1975-76, Government decided to start cadastral survey of villages which were found to be in use of the people or have become habitable and cultivable. Arrangement was made to carry out special operation in both the districts under administrative control of the respective District Councils. Generally in Assam, when it is purported to start cadastral survey in any unsurveyed part other than the Hill districts, the Assam Survey is entrusted to make field survey to ascertain the boundary of the unsurveyed area or unit called village and prepare only the map of the boundary of the concerning village or villages fixing boundary hill areas which is termed as skeleton blue prints of the village or villages. The plotwise detailed survey of the village to ascertain and draw the actual position of the plots of the village as per possession or natural features are done by land record staff and officers under Deputy Commissioner during normal period of settlement and under the Settlement Officer of the district or area, specially appointed for the purpose. This plot to plot survey and preparation of map and field survey of the concerning village is called cadastral or detail survey. Thereafter, as per existing status of an occupancy or newly offered settlement, a ledger of record of right called *Jamabandi* is prepared. The *patta* or instrument of lease according to the tenure held is offered to the tenure holder. The whole process is called the preparation of records of right and land records. This is the basic and vital process of land revenue administration. Perhaps due to difficult geographical situation and to expedite the work, instead of entrusting the work of preparation of the blue prints to the Assam Survey, a special Hill Cell Survey was established in the outskirts of Diphu town, the H.Q. of Karbi Anglong district. The process is still continuing. It is manned by experienced deputed survey officer of Assam Survey and other staff. On receipt of the blue prints from the Hill Cell Survey, settlement officers and subordinate staff and officers of both the districts, specially appointed, carry out the settlement operations for the purpose of cadastral survey, preparation and offer of record of right and assessment of revenue as per classification and use. On completion of this arduous task, land records will be prepared for present and future maintenance and revision thereof, in due course. This process will not only help in proper revenue administration of the districts but the actual and lawful occupants will enjoy their status over the land which will be the passport for protection of their legal rights over land and economic development". With regard to the progress of works relating to the cadastral survey in the district of Karbi Anglong, Chowdhury (ibid) reports that out of the total of 1399 villages taken up for the survey in the district, survey works, record attestation and revenue attestation have been completed in 1,111, 929 and 375 villages respectively.

"According to prevailing custom, the *Gaonbura* (village headman) is the custodian of the village land under the overall control of the District Council. A household is free to select a suitable plot out of the village land for its annual *jhuming* with the consent of the *Gaonbura,* but without having ownership right on that plot and such arrangement remains valid for the period of cultivation only. Flat lands suitable for wet cultivation or other permanent cultivation are, however, given allotment by the District Council to individual villagers on an annual basis. The allottee is also devoid of any right of inheritance and transfer without the prior approval of the District Council authorities." (*Project Report,* N.C. Hills District Council, 1988 : 13).

An overall idea as to the land-holding pattern prevalent in the selected IJDP centres has been attempted below on the basis of the verbal statements of the respondents at the time of field investigation.

Out of the total households of 533, the numbers of households possessing lands in the categories 0-5 *bighas** and 6-11 *bighas* are 14 (2.63%) and 154 (28.89%) respectively. The highest number of households (171) is found to have possessed lands in the category 12-17 *bighas*. In other words, 32.08% of the total households fall in this category. 109 households (20.45%) have 18-23 *bighas* while 42 households (7.88%) possess lands in the category 24-29 *bighas*. Again, 24 (4.50%) and 11 households (2.06%) possess 30-35 *bighas* and 36-41 *bighas* respectively. Only eight households (1.50%) possess more than 41 *bighas*. On the whole, it may be stated here that out of the total households of 533, 339 (63.60%) and 175 (32.83%) households possess lands in the broad categories 0-17 *bighas* and 18-35 *bighas* respectively. There are also 19 households (3.56%) possessing beyond 35 *bighas*. Table V.3 shows the land-holding pattern of the households in the selected centres.

So far as land-holding of various types is concerned, it is seen that out of the total area of 8,821 *bighas* of land, the areas under *jhum* and settled cultivation are 2,773 *bighas* (31.44%) and 3,283 *bighas* (37.22%) respectively. The area under terrace cultivation is as low as 73 *bighas* ((0.83%). The homestead land is worked out to be 1,178 *bighas* (13.35%). The area under fishery is 75 *bighas* which constitute 0.85% of the total land possessed by the households. On the other hand, the total area under horticulture is 815 *bighas*, the percentage being 9.24. The quantity of fallow land is found to be 624 *bighas* (7.07%). Thus, it is observed that the people utilise 69.49% of the total area of land in *jhum*, settled and terrace cultivation. With regard to the distribution of the cultivated land under different types, it has been observed that around 37.22% of the total land is under settled whereas 31.44% under *jhum* cultivation. The average land-holding per household and per capita land-holding have been calculated to be 16.5 *bighas* and 3.1 *bighas* respectively. A detailed break-up of the land-holding of various types in the households has been furnished in Table V.4.

Area of Land, Yield and Value of Major Crops

It has already been noted that the areas of land under *jhum*, settled and terrace cultivation are 2,773, 3,283 and 73 *bighas* respectively. The actual amount of land utilised for cultivation of crops under *jhum* cannot

---

1 bigha = 14,400 sq. ft.

be separately estimated as the people normally carry out cultivation of mixed crops in a plot of land. For this reason in Table V.5 the area of land brought under *jhum* is shown in one column against each centre, while the approximate yield and value of all the major crops usually grown in *jhum* fields are furnished in details in the corresponding columns. The table reveals that out of the total number of 533 households, the number of households engaged in *jhum* is 442 (82.9%). The yield of paddy from *jhum* fields is 5,483 quintals, the value of which accounts approximately for Rs.14,91,700.00. The quantity of maize is found to be 708 quintals and the total value is estimated at Rs.1,59,800.00. In respect of sesame cultivation, the amount of production is worked out to be 609 quintals and the value is estimated at Rs. 4,70,400.00. The category 'Others' as shown in the table includes the approximate value of the products like cotton, ginger, mustard, chilli, gourd, arum and other vegetables. The people derive an approximate amount of Rs. 3,94,100.00 for the miscellaneous products which are included in this category. Thus, it is seen that out of the three major crops viz., paddy, maize and sesame grown in the *jhum* fields, the yield of paddy is the highest followed by maize and sesame.

In the centres under investigation, out of the total households of 533, the number of households engaged in settled cultivation is found to be 473 (88.7%). The people cultivate paddy in 2758 *bighas,* mustard in 608 *bighas* and sesame in 243 *bighas* of land. The yield of paddy is 8398 quintals and the approximate value of paddy is Rs. 23,30,700.00. The yield of mustard is around 492 quintals, the approximate value of which is estimated at Rs. 2,81,800.00. Again, the production of sesame is found to be 179 quintals having a total value of around Rs.1,38,700.00. It has been observed that the people produce paddy extensively in settled cultivation. Mustard is the next important crop grown by them. On the other hand, they like to carry out cultivation of sesame in *jhum* rather than in settled field. It may also be mentioned here that the total area of land in settled cultivation is 3283 *bighas* while the total cropped area is 3609* *bighas**. This has happened due to the practice of cultivation in a particular plot of land for more than once within a calendar year. Table V.6 shows the area of land, yield and value of major crops in settled cultivation field.

The practice of terrace cultivation is found in five centres only. The number of households engaged in this cultivation is 24, the percentage being 4.5 of the total households. The area of land utilised is found to be

TABLE V.3

Land-holding Pattern of the Households in the Centres

Sl. No.	*Name of the Centres*	*Number of households possessing* 0-5 bighas	6-11 bighas	12-17 bighas	18-23 bighas	24-29 bighas	30-35 bighas	36-41 bighas	42 bighas & Above	*Total Households*
1	*2*	*3*	*4*	*5*	*6*	*7*	*8*	*9*	*10*	*11*
1	Rongbong Adong	-	25	13	4	1	-	1	1	45
2	Rongnagar	11	17	16	9	4	9	3	3	72
3	Tikaklangso	-	17	21	10	8	3	2	2	63
4	Phanglangso	-	2	29	33	1	-	-	-	65
5	Mugasong	-	8	13	1	1	-	-	-	23
6	Kaipani	1	19	25	11	1	2	1	1	61
7	Kekang Adong	-	10	15	14	4	4	2	1	50
8	Thijoklangso	-	-	9	20	18	6	1	-	54
9	Langhonjar	-	25	19	7	4	-	1	-	56
10	Recho Apam	2	31	11	-	-	-	-	-	44
	Total	14	154	171	109	42	24	11	8	533
	Percentage	2.63	28.89	32.08	20.45	7.88	4.50	2.06	1.50	99.99

73 *bighas*. The approximate yield and value of the paddy are worked out to be 246 quintals and Rs.70,900.00. respectively. In this context it may be noted here that the rates of production of paddy from *jhum,* settled and terrace cultivation are 1.98, 2.56 and 3.37 quintals per *bighas* respectively.

With regard to horticulture, it may be said that out of the total number of 533 households, 217 (40.71%) practise horticulture in 815 *bighas* of land. The approximate value of the products viz., pineapple, orange, lemon, banana, areca nut, black pepper, bay leaf and coconut etc., is found to be Rs. 2,44,900.00. Table V.7 indicates the area of land, yield and the value of terrace paddy and horticulture yield in the centres. However, it is to be noted that in respect of horticulture the yield is not shown in the table because of the fact that some of the products are not measured in quintal and the respondents, during the period of interview, simply told about the approximate amount of money received for the products.

Fishery

Fishery in the form of tank, beels* and channel etc., has been found to be possessed by only 42 (7.9%) families. The area of land covered by various types of fisheries is 75 *bighas* which constitute 0.85% of the total land possessed by the households. It has been observed that the peopld generally use the yield for the purpose of consumption only. However, in some cases, they sell fish in the nearby markets or growth centres to meet other household expenditure. The approximate amount of income derived by the people from the fisheries as per information available at the time of field investigation is to the tune of Rs. 86,600.00.

Cottage Industry

Weaving, bamboo and cane works and sericulture are the cottage industries in the area under investigation. Women are expert weavers and they weave varieties of colthes with artistic design in their looms at leisure hours. Silk worms are also reared for the purpose of weaving *eri chaddars*. On the other hand, bamboo & cane works viz., various types of baskets, mats and *murha* etc., are generally done by the menfolk at convenient time. Most of the households carry out these industries mainly for their

* *Beel* (a lake) is a local term in Assam and Bengal, used to denote low-lying marshy bodies abounded in by various aquatic fauna and flora; or in the ordinary sense of the term, a finishing ground. The land-mass of a beel is seldom used for cultivation of paddy.

TABLE V.4
Land-holding of Various Types in the Households in the Centres (in bigha)

Sl. No.	*Name of the Centres*	*No.of house-holds*	*Area of land under*			*Home-stead land*	*Land under fishery*	*Land under horti-culture*	*Fallow land*	*Total land posse-ssed*
			jhum culti-vation	*settled culti-vation*	*terrace culti-vation*					
1	*2*	*3*	*4*	*5*	*6*	*7*	*8*	*9*	*10*	*11*
1	Rongbong Adong	45	150	264	-	82	2	71	43	612
2	Rongnagar	72	387	627	-	133	21	38	84	1290
3	Tikaklangso	63	439	267	-	141	7	149	117	1120
4	Phanglangso	65	259	642	-	67	1	117	65	1151
5	Mugasong	23	87	105	3	39	2	16	46	298
6	Kaipani	61	298	328	4	198	10	56	63	957
7	Kekang Adong	50	331	224	18	134	24	138	64	933
8	Thijoklangso	54	414	379	-	205	6	194	62	1260
9	Langhonjar	56	209	322	30	127	1	22	52	763
10	Recho Apam	44	199	125	18	52	1	14	28	437
	Total	533	2773	3283	73	1178	75	815	624	8821
	Percentage		31.44	37.22	0.83	13.35	0.85	9.24	7.07	100.00

TABLE V.5

Areaof Jhum Lanc., Yield and Value of Major Crops

Land- In Bigha
Yield - In Quintal
Value - Rs. in Thousand

Sl. No.	Name of the Centres	Total house-holds	No.of house-holds having jhum	Total area of land	Paddy		Maize		Sesame		Value	Total Value
					Yield	Value	Yield	Value	Yield	Value	Value	
1	2	3	4	5	6	7	8	9	10	11	12	13
1	Rongbong Adong	45	33	150	285	85.5	43	8.6	41	30.8	39.1	164.0
2	Rongnagar	72	57	387	697	174.2	91	22.8	72	57.6	64.0	318.6
3	Tikaklangso	63	57	439	882	220.5	96	24.0	94	70.5	54.7	369.7
4	Phanglangso	65	48	259	475	142.5	82	16.4	61	45.8	33.8	238.8
5	Mugasong	23	15	87	182	54.6	21	5.2	24	19.2	15.5	94.5
6	Kaipani	61	49	298	581	174.3	81	16.2	71	56.8	36.9	284.2
7	Kekang Adong	50	45	331	671	167.7	74	18.5	57	42.8	38.4	267.4
8	Thijoklangso	54	51	414	812	203.0	82	20.5	87	65.3	39.8	328.6
9	Langhonjar	56	46	209	471	141.3	71	14.2	53	42.4	37.2	235.1
10	Recho Apam	44	41	199	427	128.1	67	13.4	49	39.2	34.7	215.4
	Total	533	422	2773	5483	1491.7	708	159.8	609	470.4	394.1	2516.6

N.B. – The coloum 'others' includes cotton, ginger, mustard, chilli and vegetables etc.

TABLE V.6

Area of Land, Yield and Value of Major Crops in Settled Cultivation

Land - In Bigha
Yield - In Quintal
Value - Rs. in '000'

Sl. No.	Name of the Centres	Total house holds	No.of -households having settled cultivation	Total area of land	Paddy			Mustard			Sesame			Total value	Total cropped area
					Area of land	Yield	value	Area of land	Yield	value	Area of land	Yield	value		
1	2	3	4	5	6	7	8	9	10	11	12	13	14	15	16
1	Rongbong Adong	45	37	264	207	579	173.7	81	61	33.6	25	18	13.5	220.8	313
2	Rongnagar	72	69	627	517	1548	387.0	128	103	61.8	38	27	21.6	470.4	683
3	Tikaklangso	63	47	267	235	726	181.5	54	45	24.8	19	14	10.5	216.8	308
4	Phanglangso	65	62	642	558	1674	502.2	81	69	37.9	33	26	19.5	559.6	672
5	Mugasong	23	21	105	78	240	72.0	28	23	13.8	9	7	5.6	91.4	115
6	Kaipani	61	50	328	300	885	265.5	57	44	26.4	34	25	20.0	311.9	391
7	Kekang Adong	50	45	224	186	596	149.0	42	34	13.7	16	12	9.0	176.7	244
8	Thijoklangso	54	50	379	292	905	226.3	75	60	33.0	26	19	14.2	273.5	393
9	Langhonjar	56	53	322	281	893	267.9	37	32	19.2	24	17	13.6	300.7	342
10	Recho Apam	44	39	125	104	352	105.6	25	21	12.6	19	14	11.2	129.4	148
	Total	533	473	3283	2758	8398	2330.7	608	492	281.8	243	179	138.7	2751.2	3609

TABLE V.7

Area of Land, Yield and Value of Terrace Paddy and Horticulture Yield

Land- In Bigha
Yield - In Quintal
Value - Rs. in Thousand

Sl. No.	Name of the Centres	Total house-holds	No.of house-holds having terrace	Terrace Paddy			No.of house-holds having horticulture	Horticulture yield		
				Area of land	Yield	Value		Area of land	value	Total value
1	2	3	4	5	6	7	8	9	10	11
1	Rongbong Adong	45	-	-	-	-	25	71	37.5	261.0
2	Rongnagar	72	-	-	-	-	17	38	11.9	468.3
3	Tikaklangso	63	-	-	-	-	28	149	37.2	244.5
4	Phanglangso	65	-	-	-	-	42	117	29.9	608.3
5	Mugasong	23	3	3	10	3.0	9	16	6.4	103.9
6	Kaipani	61	3	4	13	3.9	21	56	15.6	308.1
7	Kekang Adong	50	2	18	58	14.5	25	138	38.7	220.7
8	Thijoklangso	54	-	-	-	-	32	194	54.5	353.2
9	Langhonjar	56	9	30	103	30.9	12	22	7.5	326.1
10	Recho Apam	44	7	18	62	18.6	6	14	5.7	137.9
	Total	533	24	73	246	70.9	217	815	244.9	3032.0

TABLE V.8

Distribution of Livestock Population in the Area of Study

Sl. No.	Name of the Centres	Bullock	Cow	Buffalo	Goat	Pig	Poultry	Total
1	2	3	4	5	6	7	8	9
1	Rongbong Adong	42	35	10	38	74	350	549
2	Rongnagar	96	92	24	75	116	516	889
3	Tikaklangso	74	36	12	32	85	412	651
4	Phanglangso	85	41	16	57	123	325	647
5	Mugasong	26	19	6	31	46	61	189
6	Kaipani	64	45	14	42	-	56	221
7	Kekang Adong	52	37	18	25	86	120	338
8	Thijoklangso	74	58	12	52	107	250	553
9	Langhonjar	38	25	46	27	115	375	625
10	Recho Apam	24	21	32	35	86	218	416
	Total	575	379	190	414	838	2683	5079
	Percentage	11.32	7.46	3.74	8.15	16.50	52.83	100.00

TABLE V.9

Gross annual income of the households from various sources

(Rs. in '000')

Sl. No.	Name of the Centres	Total house-holds	Total members	Income from (Rs. in Thousand) Land	Live stock	Fishery	Cottage Industry	Contract/ Business	Paid employ-ment inclu-ding daily wage	Total Income	Income per house-hold	Per capita Income
1	*2*	*3*	*4*	*5*	*6*	*7*	*8*	*9*	*10*	*11*	*12*	*13*
1	Rongbong Adong	45	246	422.3	35.1	2.1	29.6	-	53.1	542.2	12048	2204
2	Rongnagar	72	442	800.9	63.6	16.5	65.7	76.5	186.2	1209.4	16797	2736
3	Tikaklangso	63	306	623.7	32.5	9.4	41.1	-	45.3	752.0	11936	2457
4	Phanglangso	65	296	828.0	63.2	2.5	41.5	-	46.8	982.0	15107	3317
5	Mugasong	23	106	195.3	11.8	1.6	14.1	-	43.6	266.4	11582	2513
6	Kaipani	61	325	615.6	39.5	12.7	47.9	-	31.2	746.9	12244	2298
7	Kekang Adong	50	231	497.3	35.9	28.4	31.8	125.1	127.4	845.9	16918	3661
8	Thijoklangso	54	240	656.6	36.5	9.7	33.6	11.6	38.2	786.1	14557	3275
9	Langhonjar	56	409	574.2	47.6	2.5	46.1	-	36.5	706.9	12623	1728
10	Recho Apam	44	264	369.1	42.4	1.2	39.8	-	32.7	485.2	11027	1837
	Total	533	2865	5583.0	408.1	86.6	391.2	213.2	640.9	7323.0	13739	2556
	Percentage			76.24	5.57	1.18	5.34	2.91	8.75	99.99		

own consumption. Raw materials are purchased from the local markets and some of them are also collected from the forests. The investigation reveals that the people have derived income amounting to Rs. 3,91,200.00 out of the above mentioned products of the cottage industries.

Livestock

The people possess domesticated animals and birds like bullock, buffalo, cow, goat, pig and poultry etc. Buffalo and bullock are primarily meant for agricultural operations in the low-lying areas. Rearing of pig and poultry is a common sight in the area because of the fact that the people generally utilise them not only for domestic consumption but also for offering worship to various deities. Sometimes surplus quantities are sold in the local markets to supplement their cash earning. Table V.8 shows the distribution of the livestock population in the field. It is seen that out of a total of 5,079, the number of poultry (2,683) is the highest. In terms of percentage it is 52.83 of the total livestock. Bullocks with 575 numbers constitute 11.32% while 379 cows constitute 7.46% only. It may be pointed out here that the people are not usually habituated in taking milk and as such they do not show much inclination in domesticating cows. The number of buffaloes is found to be 190 (3.74%). There are also 838 pigs and 414 goats which account for 16.50% and 8.15% respectively. On the whole, it may be stated here that the role played by domestic animals and birds in the economy of the people is not negligible. The study reveals that the people derive approximately an amount of Rs. 4,08,100.00 out of the livestock population.

Annual Income

The general experience of a social researcher in generating data on the total income of a population is not encouraging. Very often it may not be possible to rely entirely on the stated figures relating to the total income of a family from all possible sources. The problem becomes more acute when no authentic counter-checks are available for the purpose. The respondents may be quite honestly ignorant of the actual income of the family or may deliberately mis-state the figures.

In the present population, the main source of income is agriculture. In some cases, however, it is supplemented by jobs, wage earning, business and some other sources. In most of the cases, the annual earnings could not be collected with hundred percent accuracy. Approximate figures in these regards were recorded on the basis of personal observation and the checked and counter-checked information obtained from the neighbouring families. Little bit of variations in the figures, however, are not likely to have much reflection on the overall economic picture of the people, drawn out of the present study.

A detailed account of the people's income from various sources as well as their total and per capita income has been presented in Table V.9. The table reveals that the average annual income of a household is Rs.13,739.00 and the per capita annual income is Rs. 2,556.00. The per capita income ranges from Rs.1,728.00 (Langhonjar Centre) to Rs.3,661.00 (Kekang Adong Centre). The table further reveals that the people derive the major portion (76.24%) of their income, as noted earlier, from agriculture. The income from livestock also contributes a reasonable amount towards the maintenance of the households. They derive 5.57% of the total income from livestock population. 'Paid employment including daily wages' contributes 8.75% of the income and 2.91% income is derived from contract works and other business sources. The rest of the income is derived from the means like cottage industry (5.34%) and fishery (1.18%) etc.

Annual Expenditure

In case of data regarding the annual expenditure of the households too, it is quite possible that a respondent may not be able to recapitulate the actual amount of expenditure incurred on various items throughout the year. As such, the figures shown in Table V.10 do not necessarily mean the exact amount of expenditure but however, provide us with an overall pattern of annual expenditure of the people. It is evident from the table that food is the only major head of expenditure constituting 63.25% of the total expenses of a family. The amount of expenditure in dress and ornaments is worked out to be 4.10%. The percentage of expenditure is found to be 4.70 only in respect of education. This is probably indicative of the people's relatively lesser importance towards education of their children. Again, they spend 3.90% of the total expenditure for treatment of diseases. In this context, it may relevantly be noted here that the people take little interest in medicare system. The percentage of expenditure on the items like betel nut, tobacco and beverage etc., is 4.20. In case of travelling and transport the expenditure is 3.65%. The amount of expenditure incurred by the families is 2.90% for festivals and ceremonies while it is 1.40% for other social obligations. They generally spend around 2.26% of

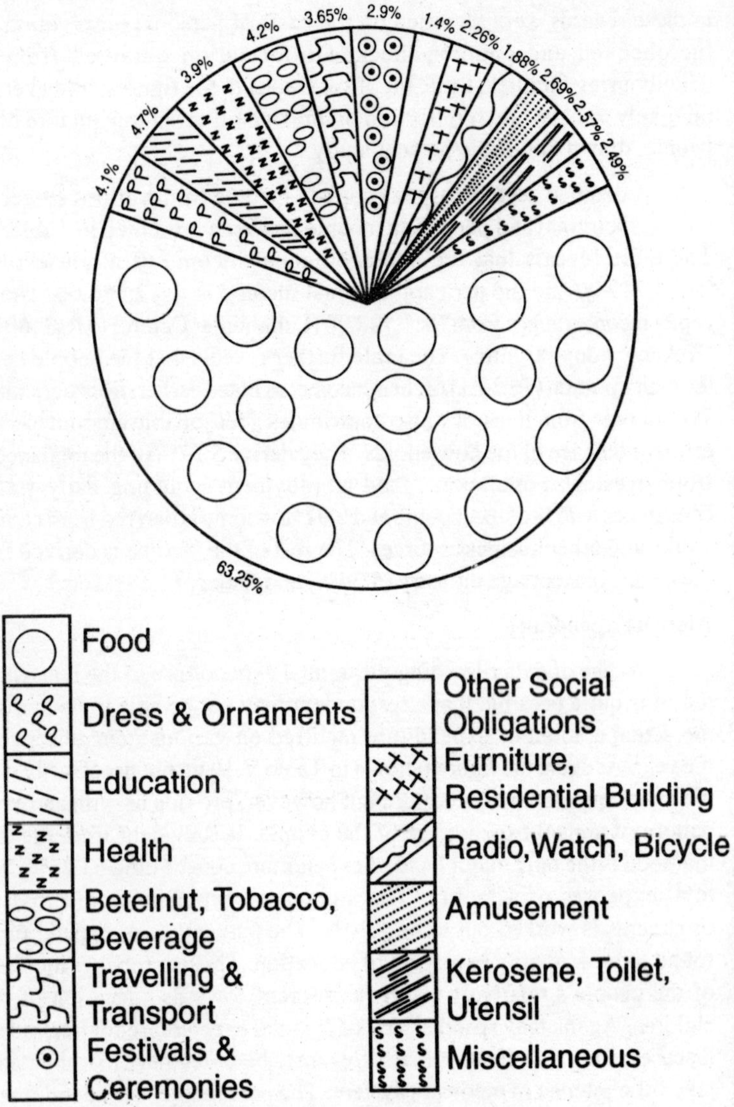

Fig. 4. Pie Diagram showing the Pattern of Annual Expenditure of the Households

TABLE V.10

Average Annual Expenditure of the Households

(Rs. in Thousand)

Sl. No.	Name of the Centres	Total house-holds	No. of members	Expenditure on different items: Food	Dress & Ornaments	Educ-ation	Health	Betel nut, Tobacco, Beverage	Trave-lling & Trans-port	Festi-vals & cere-monies
1	2	3	4	5	6	7	8	9	10	11
1	Rongbong Adong	45	246	315.6	24.5	18.5	19.7	23.2	17.6	13.2
2	Rongnagar	72	442	668.3	51.6	65.3	55.8	53.6	45.9	44.2
3	Tikaklangso	63	306	435.2	25.8	31.7	28.3	33.7	26.5	19.2
4	Phanglangso	65	296	612.8	35.1	26.8	32.7	43.8	31.2	32.7
5	Mugasong	23	106	157.6	10.8	14.2	11.1	10.9	9.2	6.1
6	Kaipani	61	325	436.1	24.7	28.6	22.4	29.8	25.3	18.6
7	Kekang Adong	50	231	476.3	34.8	46.2	35.7	34.6	31.4	23.5
8	Thijoklangso	54	240	444.6	31.5	52.8	36.5	28.7	34.2	22.3
9	Langhonjar	56	409	486.2	25.7	20.3	16.2	19.2	18.4	13.1
10	Recho Apam	44	264	330.9	18.3	19.6	10.5	12.6	12.3	7.2
	Total	533	2865	4363.6	282.8	324.0	268.9	290.1	252.0	200.1
	Percentage			63.25	4.10	4.70	3.90	4.20	3.65	2.90

continued ....

TABLE V.10

Average Annual Expenditure of the Households

(Rs. in Thousnad)

Sl. No.	Name of the Centres	*Expenditure on different items* Other social oblig-ations	Furni-ture, Residential building	Radio, Watch Bicycle	Amusement	Kerosene, Toilet, Utensil	Misce-llaneous	Total expen-diture	Per capita expen-diture
		12	*13*	*14*	*15*	*16*	*17*	*18*	*19*
1	Rongbong Adong	6.3	15.2	9.4	17.1	14.3	16.2	510.8	2076
2	Rongnagar	23.5	22.4	21.6	32.7	25.3	32.1	1142.3	2584
3	Tikaklangso	9.2	21.3	14.6	21.1	18.2	21.7	706.5	2308
4	Phanglangso	10.1	14.5	16.8	21.3	21.6	22.4	921.8	3114
5	Mugasong	2.2	4.2	4.1	7.1	7.5	6.4	251.4	2371
6	Kaipani	9.5	27.5	16.8	21.4	23.5	18.5	702.7	2162
7	Kekang Adong	10.6	21.3	18.5	24.8	19.2	21.4	798.3	3455
8	Thijoklangso	9.7	12.5	12.6	21.4	17.8	17.1	741.7	3090
9	Langhonjar	8.5	9.2	9.7	11.9	19.3	9.3	667.0	1630
10	Recho Apam	7.1	7.5	5.8	7.1	10.9	6.7	456.5	1729
	Total	96.7	155.6	129.9	185.9	177.6	171.8	6899.0	2708
	Percentage	1.40	2.26	1.88	2.69	2.57	2.49	99.99	

the total expenditure in connection with furniture and residential building etc. Again, radio, watch and bicycle etc., are purchased or repaired for which 1.88% expenditure is incurred. The amount of expenditure is 2.69% in amusement and 2.57% in kerosene, toilet items and utensils etc. The miscellaneous expenditure has been calculated to be 2.49%. On the whole, the average annual expenditure of a household is Rs.12,943.00 against the average annual income of Rs.13,739.00. Thus, it seems, on the average a household is having a marginal surplus budget of Rs.796.00 per annum. Again, per capita expenditure has been worked out to be Rs.2,408.00 against per capita income of Rs. 2,556.00. It is, therefore, seen that there is a very meagre per capita surplus of Rs.148.00 per annum. It is thus apparent that the people under investigation, by and large have been living in a subsistence level economy.

It may not be out of place to mention here that out of the total number of 533 househlods, 184 households with a total population of 991 are living below poverty line (Rupees Eleven Thousand and less). In other words, 34.5% of the total households are still living below the poverty line. The number of households living below poverty line is furnished centrewise: Rongbong Adong-14, Rongnagar- 19, Tikaklangso -25, Phanglangso-20, Mugasong-7, Kaipani-24, Kekang Adong-12, Thijoklangso- 21, Langhonjar-24 and Recho Apam-18. It should be noted here that at the time of the preparation of the Project Report for implementing the schemes under the IJDP, the Karbi Anglong Autonomous Council, Diphu considered all the households to be living below poverty line, although there were some households living above the line. However, it may be assumed that a sizeable section of the households have been able to augment their economic condition. It may be relevantly noted here that the percentages of population lying below the poverty line in the seven States of North-east India *(The Assam Tribune,* March 10, 1997) are: Assam-40.86%, Arunachal Pradesh -39.35%, Tripura-39.02%, Meghalaya-37.92%, Nagaland-37.92%, Manipur-33.78 and Mizoram-25.66%.

Category of Beneficiary Households

The investigation reveals that out of 533 households, 442 (82.93%) are *jhumias*. Again, the households practising *jhum* partially are 382 (71.67%) while those practising fully are 60 (11.26%). The number of non-*jhumias* is 91 (17.07%). In spite of the implementation of various schemes under the IJDP, the percentageof non-*jhumias* appears to be relatively less. But it should be kept in mind that the families practising *jhum* fully are also less in number. On the other hand, the number of households practising *jhum* partially is relatively more. This indicates that the people do not depend mainly on *jhum* lands but also practise settled cultivation for their livelihood. Table V.11 shows the distribution of *jhumias* and non-*jhumias* in the centres.

IJDP Schemes

A good number of schemes have been implemented under the *Integrated Jhumia Development Programme* in the studied centres during the period of five years (1986-87 to 1990-91). Land development, supply of agricultural input, horticultural assistance, supply of bullocks and piggery units, water distribution, fishery, supply of loom sets and sewing machines and provision of rubber cultivation etc., are the major schemes implemented in the area.

Land Development

"One of the main objectives of the IJDP is to provide developed land fit for permanent cultivation to the *jhumia* families. The Agriculture Department's Engineering Wing and the Soil Conservation Department are entrusted with the schemes for developing the land which includes levelling or terracing and provision of irrigation facilities. Within the ambit of IJDP schemes water of the streams/springs will be tapped for irrigation of the terraced land. Considering the terrain gradient of the hills and distances of the water course, a family will be given one hectare of developed irrigated land. For this purpose, lands have been identified in the vicinity of the *jhumia's* habitation within a Project Centre for development and distribution amongst the local tribal families of the Project Centre by the Karbi Anglong District Council" (Karbi Anglong District Council, 1988 : 36).

Table V.12 provides an idea about the land development in the centres under study. It will be seen from the table that out of 10 centres, 7 (70%) have been covered by this scheme. The scheme has been implemented for a period of five years in one centre only. Again, in two centres it has been implemented for four consecutive years. Out of the remaining four centres, 1, 2 and 1 centres have been provided with this scheme for 3, 2 and 1 years respectively. However, in one centre, an approach road measuring 5 km has also been constructed for the convenience of the people. It may also

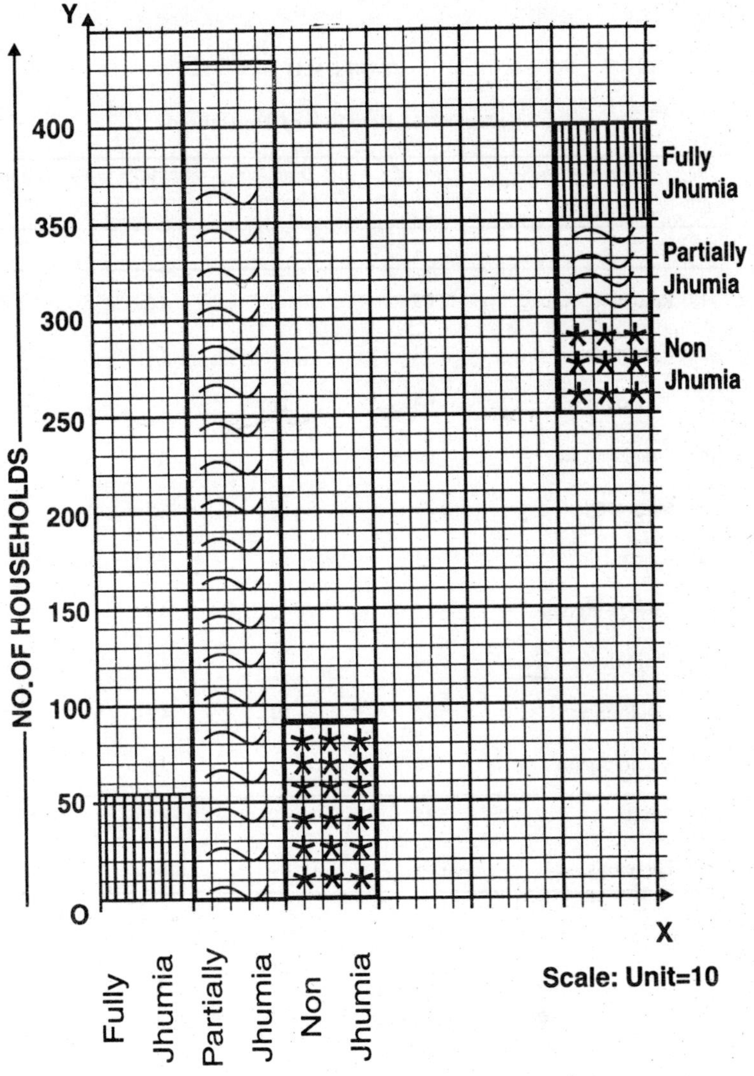

Fig. 5. Histogram showing the Category of Households

TABLE V.11

Category of Beneficiary Households

Sl. No.	*Name of the Centres*	*No. of households*	*Fully jhumia*	*Partially jhumia*	*Non-jhumia*
1	*2*	*3*	*4*	*5*	*6*
1	Rongbong Adong	45	8	25	12
2	Rongnagar	72	3	54	15
3	Tikaklangso	63	16	41	6
4	Phanglangso	65	3	45	17
5	Mugasong	23	2	13	8
6	Kaipani	61	11	38	12
7	Kekang Adong	50	5	40	5
8	Thijoklangso	54	4	47	3
9	Langhonjar	56	3	43	10
10	Recho Apam	44	5	36	3
	Total	533	60	382	91
	Percentage	100.00	11.26	71.67	17.07

be mentioned here that water distribution scheme has been implemented in seven centres to enhance agricultural production.

Agricultural Input

In order to motivate the people thoroughly towards settled mode of cultivation, the agricultural scheme has been implemented by the concerned Department in the centres. Paddy, mustard, maize, sesame and vegetable seeds etc., have been supplied to the people. In addition, fertilizer, compost, pesticide and small agricultural implements have also been supplied to them free of cost. Table V.13 shows the various items of agricultural input supplied to the people of the centres. It is seen from the table that out of the ten centres, 7 have been provided with seeds of various crops. One centre has received seeds for four consecutive years while another centre has received seeds for two years. Again, two centres have received different kinds of agricultural seeds for one year. The remaining three centres have been provided with one or two varieties of seeds for one year only. The table further reveals that five centres have received fertilizers, compost and pesticides for having a better yield. Again, small agricultural implements viz., spade, sickle, *dao,* garden rake, plough and hand sprayer etc., have been supplied to the people of nine centres to enable them to carry out agricultural activities smoothly.

Horticultural Assistance

So far as horticultural assistance is concerned, it is seen that out of the ten centres, six have received horticultural input. Pineapple suckers have been supplied to six centres sufficiently. Orange seedling and Assam lemon have been provided to four centres while coconut seedlings and black pepper cuttings have been provided to two centres. Moreover, arecanut, *leteku,* bay leaf, mango, litchi and papaya etc., have also been supplied to some centres in some quantities to draw the attention of the people towards horticultural activities. Table V.14 shows horticultural assistance provided to the people in different years.

Veterinary Input

Rearing of animals and birds is a part of the traditional culture of the Karbis. They sacrifice pigs and poultry to appease various deities. However, the Department of Animal Husbandry & Veterinary has implemented the scheme of supplying bullocks, milch cows and pigs in the IJDP centres. Table V.15 shows the distribution of the livestock in the

TABLE V.12

Land development under IJDP in the centres during 1986-91

Sl. No.	*Name of the Centres*	*Year*	*Land Development (in ha.)*
1	*2*	*3*	*4*
1	Rongbong Adong	1986-87	(i) 5 (ii) 5 km. (Road)
2	Rongnagar	1986-91	NIL
3	Tikaklangso	1986-87	11
		1987-88	3
4	Phanglangso	1986-87	10
		1987-88	40
5	Mugasong	1986-87	15
		1987-88	11
		1988-89	23
6	Kaipani	1986-87	16
		1987-88	24
		1988-89	18
		1989-90	16
		1990-91	21
7	Kekang Adong	1986-91	NIL
8	Thijoklangso	1986-91	NIL
9	Langhonjar	1986-87	20
		1987-88	20
		1988-89	30
		1989-90	20
10	Recho Apam	1986-87	14
		1987-88	20
		1988-89	20
		1989-90	25

TABLE V.13

Agricultural input supplied to the centres under IJDP during 1986-91

Sl. No.	Name of the Centres	Year	Seeds	Quantity (q)	Agricultural Input: Fertilizer	Quantity	Implements	Quantity
1	2	3	4	5	6	7	8	9
1	Rongbong Adong	1986-87	(i) Paddy	12.00	(i) Compost	15 q	(i) Implements	90 sets
			(ii) Wheat	1.50	(ii) Pesticides	4 ltrs	(ii) Hand sprayer	3 nos.
			(iii) Ginger	15.00				
			(iv) Mustard	2.30				
			(v) Sesame	1.77				
			(vi) Veg. seeds	1.04				
		1989-90	(i) Mustard	14.16	(i) Aldrex	36 kgs		
			(ii) Potato seeds	70.80	(ii) Diathene M-45	2 kg		
			(iii) Veg. seeds	118 kits				
2	Rongnagar	1986-87	(i) Paddy	4.00	(i) Pesticides	20 ltrs.	(i) Implements	39 sets
			(ii)Mustard	5.00				
		1987-88	(i) Paddy	10.00				
			(ii) Ginger	78.00				
			(iii) Veg. seeds	360 pkts.				

Continued ....

1	2	3	4	5	6	7	8	9
		1988-89	(i) Turmeric rhizomes	26.00				
		1989-90	(i) Maize	1.20	(i) Urea	20.35 q	(i) Hand sprayer	2 nos.
			(ii) Sesame	0.20	(ii) S.S.P.	13.30 q		
			(iii) Onion	0.12	(iii) MOP	5.85 q		
			(iv) Chilli	0.05	(iv) FYM	50 Tonnes		
			(v) Garlic	2.27	(v) Rogor	250 M		
			(vi) Corriander	0.10	(vi) HYM	82 MT		
					(vii) Aldrex	0.25		
					(vii) Diathene	0.01		
3	Tikaklangso	1986-91	-	-	-	-	-	-
4	Phanglangso	1990-91	-	-	-	-	(i) Spade	140 nos.
							(ii) Sickle	140 nos.
							(iii) Dao	140 nos.
							(iv) Garden rake	140 nos.
							(v) M.B. plough	70 nos.
							(vi) Hand sprayer	4 nos.

Continued ....

TABLE V.13
Argicultural input supplied to the centres under IJDP during 1986-91

1	2	3	4	5	6	7	8	9
5	Mugasong	1989-90	-	-	-	-	(i) Plough	29 nos.
							(ii) Spade	116 nos.
							(iii) Sickle	58 nos.
							(iv) Dao	68 nos.
							(v) Garden rake	58 nos.
							(vi) Paddy weeders	8 nos.
							(vii) Hand sprayer	14 nos.
							(viii) M.B. plough	24 nos.
6	Kaipani	1989-90	(i) Paddy	6.00	-	-	(i) Garden rake	60 nos.
			(ii) Ginger	45.00			(ii) Spade	96 nos.
			(iii) Sesame	2.40			(iii) Axe	60 nos.
			(iv) Turmeric	30.00			(iv) Dao	60 nos.
			(v) Mustard	3.60			(v) Khupri	60 nos.
			(vi) Maize	12.00				
7	Kekang Adong	1986-87	-	-	-	-	(i) Implements	50 sets
							(ii) Hand sprayer	1 no.
		1990-91	(i) Ginger	60.00	-	-	-	-

Continued ....

1	2	3	4	5	6	7	8	9
8	Thijoklangso	1986-87	-	-	-	-	(i) Implements	100 sets
							(i) Hand sprayer	1no.
		1989-90	(i) Mustard	4.40	(i) MOP	2.60	(i) Hand sprayer	4nos.
					(ii) Urea	36.90	(ii) Plastic bucket	30 nos.
					(iii) Diathene	1.19		
					(iv) Anusar	1.00		
9	Langhonjar	1986-87	(i) Paddy	4.80	(i) Pesticides	5 ltrs	(i) Implements	48 sets
			(ii) Mustard	0.96			(ii) Hand sprayer	4 nos.
			(iii) Maize	4.80				
			(iv) Ginger	24.00				
			(v) Veg.seeds	96 kits				
10	Recho Apam	1986-87	(i) Paddy	13.20	(i) Anusar	1 q	(i) Implements	55 sets
			(ii) Veg. seeds	121 kits			(ii) Hand sprayer	2nos.

TABLE V.14

Horticultural assistance under IJDP

Sl. No.	Name of the Centres	Year	Items		Quantity (No.)
1	2	3	4		5
1	Rongbong Adong	1986-87	(i)	Pineapple suckers	75,000
			(ii)	Assam Lemon	2,250
			(iii)	Leteku	90
			(iv)	Big leaf	140
			(v)	Coconut seedings	110
			(vi)	Mango	100
			(vii)	Orange	200
			(viii)	Arecanut	1,000
		1988-89		Pineapple Suckers	39,000
		1989-90		Pineapple Suckers	1,71,000
2	Rongnagar	1986-87	(i)	Pineapple Suckers	39,000
			(ii)	Litchi	200
			(iii)	Arecanut	4,440
			(iv)	Papaya	300
		1989-90	(i)	Arecanut	1,440
			(ii)	Bay leaf	720
			(iii)	Black pepper cuttings	720
3	Tikaklangso	1986-91		-	-
4	Phanglangso	1986-91		-	-
5	Mugasong	1986-91		-	-
6	Kaipani	1989-90	(i)	Pineapple suckers	30,000
			(ii)	Arecanut	3,000

continued.................

1	2	3	4		5
7	Kekang Adong	1986-87	(i)	Pineapple suckers	4,25,000
			(ii)	Assam lemon	2,000
			iii)	Orange	6,800
		1989-90	(i)	Orange seedlings	24,900
			(ii)	Assam lemon	18,200
8	Thijoklangso	1986-87	(i)	Pineapple suckers	4,25,000
			(ii)	Assam lemon	2,000
			(iii)	Orange	6,800
9	Langhonjar	1986-87	(i)	Pineapple suckers	48,000
			(ii)	Assam lemon	240
			(iii)	Orange	960
			(iv)	Coconut seedlings	240
			(v)	Bay leaf	240
			(vi)	Black pepper cuttings	450
10	Recho Apam	1986-91			

area. It will be seen from the table that altogether 70 pair of bullocks have been supplied to the people of five centres. Again, 20 units* of pig have been supplied to the people of two centres during 1990-91. It may be noted here that milch cows have not been distributed among the people.

Pisciculture

Although there is dearth of suitable land for pisciculture in the hilly areas, the Department of Fisheries has developed several fisheries in the centres for the benefit of the people. Table V.16 indicates the distribution of fisheries in the centres. The table reveals that out of the total number of ten centres, 7 have been provided with a total of 10 fisheries. There are also three centres having two fisheries each.

Other Schemes

Weaving is an important cottage industry among the Karbis. Every woman is a born weaver. She knows how to weave beautiful clothes in the traditional loom which, of course, involves maximum labour and time. In order to remove these difficulties the Department of Handloom and Textiles has supplied fly shuttle looms with all accessories, cotton yarn and C.I. sheet for construction of loom shed in two centres. The Rongbong Adong centre has received 5 while the Rongnagar centre has received 39 loom sets during 1986-87.

Similarly, the Department of Industries has provided sewing machines with all accessories to two centres. The Kekang Adong and Thijoklangso centres have received 20 sewing machines, each during 1987-88.

The scheme of rubber plantation has been implemented in two centres. The plantation has been started at Phanglangso centre in a plot of land measuring 20 hectares during the period 1988-89 and at Kaipani in an area of 5 hectares during 1989-90.

Bamboo plantation has been carried out in two centres. Lands measuring 10 hectares and 15 hectares have been brought under bamboo plantation during 1990-91 in Langhonjar and Recho Apam centres respectively.

In order to promote ecology and to increase supply of fuelwood to the people the Social Forestry scheme has been implemented in two centres. These are Phanglangso and Kaipani.

---

* One units of pig consists of one male and two females.

TABLE V.15

Veterinary Input in the Centres

Sl. No.	*Name of the Centres*	*Year*	*Items*
1	*2*	*3*	*4*
1	Rongbong Adong	1988-89	Bullock 3 pair
		1990-91	Bullock 10 pair
2	Rongnagar	1990-91	Bullock 10 pair
3	Tikaklangso	1990-91	Bullock 12 pair
4	Phanglangso	1986-91	-
5	Mugasong	1986-91	-
6	Kaipani	1986-91	-
7	Kekang Adong	1987-88	Piggery 10 units
		1990-91	Bullock 20 pair
8	Thijoklangso	1987-88	Piggery 10 units
		1990 -91	Bullock 15 pair
9	Langhonjar	1986-91	-
10	Recho Apam	1986-91	-

TABLE V.16

Pisciculture input in the centres

Sl. No.	*Name of the Centres*	*Year*	*Fishery (No.)*
1	*2*	*3*	*4*
1	Rongbong Adong	1987-88	1
		1988-89	1
2	Rongnagar	1986-87	1
3	Tikaklangso	1986-91	-
4	Phanglangso	1988-89	1
5	Mugasong	1986-91	-
6	Kaipani	1986-91	-
7	Kekang Adong	1987-88	1
8	Thijoklangso	1988-89	1
9	Langhonjar	1990-91	2
10	Recho Apam	1990-91	2
	Total		10

Moreover, a training for the farmers with 45 participants has also been organised at Rongbong Adong centre during 1986-87.

It may be pointed out here that the following officers have been appointed as Project Officers for smooth implementation of the IJDP schemes in the district of Karbi Anglong :

1. Divisional Officer, Soil Conservation, Diphu
2. Divisional Officer, Soil Conservation, Kohora
3. Divisional Officer, Soil Conservation, Hamren
4. Superintendent, Sericulture, Hamren
5. Superintendent, Handloom & Textiles, Diphu
6. Executive Engineer (Irrigation), Mechanical, Bokulia
7. District Agricultural Officer, Diphu
8. Superintendent, Weaving, Diphu
9. District Veterinary & Animal Husbandry Officer, Diphu

On the whole, it may be said that all efforts have been made by the Government as well as the District Council, Diphu to motivate the *jhumias* towards settled mode of livelihood and to wean them away from the shifting cultivation. From the point of view of the *jhumias* inhabiting the IJDP centres, it may be mentioned here that the people have realised the importance of the schemes and have tried to derive benefits out of them as far as practicable. The increase of non-*jhumias* in proportion to *jhumias* fully involved in *jhum* probably indicates a favourable and positive trend towards the adoption of the welfare schemes by the people. Moreover, the number of households living above the poverty line is also increasing considerably although the average annual income of the households does not seem to be very satisfactory. The impact of the different schemes on the *jhumias* inhabiting the centres will, however, be highlighted in the next chapter.

VI

IMPACT OF THE PROGRAMME ON THE PEOPLE

In the preceding chapter the various welfare schemes implemented under the *Integrated Jhumia Development Programme* (IJDP) during the period of five years from 1986-87 to 1990-91 in the studied centres of Karbis Anglong have been discussed in details. In this chapter an attempt is being made to assess the impact of the *jhum* control schemes under the IJDP on the hill Karbis who constitute the only ethnic group in the centres.

At the very outset, it should be submitted that despite all possible efforts sufficient authentic quantitative data in this regard could not be generated from the field for some obvious constraints. Because of their low literacy level as well as because of their ignorance as to the exact amount of different types of land possessed by them, most of the people could not provide very authentic data in these regards. The discussion, therefore, has by and large been confined to the qualitative aspect of the impact as a whole. Some illustrative quantified data have, however, been incorporated here and there while referring to some specific instances.

The IJDP seems to be a very popular term among the people. The villagers by and large have been found to be in the knowledge of the programme. Level of education of the people has not been an impediment in this awareness. However, the degree and the extent of their knowledge about the programme have some positive correlation with educational attainment. A number of factors might have contributed towards this observed mass-awareness of the programme. The important ones include (i) A village level development committee has been formed in each IJDP centre. The president and the secretary have been selected from the centre itself so that there is more communication and interaction between the implementing agencies and the beneficiaries ; (ii) All the households of a centre have been taken into account as beneficiaries of the schemes implemented in the centre. This, however, does not mean that every household has received assistance in an equal manner. For instance, a household may not avail benefit under Land Development scheme, but it has received assistance from other schemes. Thus, all the households of a centre in some way have been involved with the task of controlling *jhum* and as a result, much awareness about the programme has developed at the grass root level; (iii) The people are economically very backward. The practice of *jhum* cannot provide them with food necessary for the whole year. As a matter of fact, they have to search for the forest products viz., edible roots and tubers etc., during the lean months of the year for their livelihood. Moreover, they generally come down to the plains areas and come into contact with various sections of the people and observe vast difference in the standard of living. As such, they themselves were already thinking of some alternative means of livelihood. Consequently, when they came to know about the implementation of the IJDP, the people, by and large, showed keen interest without any hesitation.

It may relevantly be noted here that the different schemes under the IJDP have not been equally implemented in all the centres. Thus, for example, the schemes like Land Development, supply of Agricultural Input and Pisciculture have been provided to seven centres out of the total number of ten centres while Horticultural Assistance have been provided to six centres. Again, Bullocks and Pigs have been supplied to the people of five centres and two centres respectively. Fly Shuttle Looms with accessories and Sewing Machines have been provided to two centres only. In spite of the differential implementation of the schemes, it has been observed that these have been able to draw a sincere attention of the people towards harmful effects of the shifting cultivation.

Land Development is one of the major schemes under the IJDP. The scheme comprises bench terracing, land reclamation, land levelling and graded bunding including provision of irrigation facilities. Details of activities under this scheme have already been furnished in Table V.12. During the present investigation it has been reported by the respondents of Tikaklangso centre that they have been benefitted by this scheme to a great extent. The beneficiaries have cultivated the plots of land made suitable for cultivation by the concerned department and they have received satisfactory yields. On the other hand, the people of Mugasong centre are not happy over the implementation of the scheme. The original plot of land reclaimed by the concerned department was not suitable for agricultural activities due to sterile condition of the soil. However, the department reclaimed another plot of land and provided with irrigation facilities. But the people did not carry out cultivation for the reason that the temporary irrigation facilities made availlable by the department became nonoperative by heavy current of water. Thus, it seems that all the targetted people could not derive the desired benefits out of the scheme in spite of a substantial amount of money and organisational efforts being involved in the process. As a matter of fact, the effective implementation of a scheme primarily depends on the efficiency of the village level development committee in general and the village level IJDP secretary in particular. The secretary is in a sense the link personnel between the government departments including Project Office of the District Council and the village people. The investigation further reveals that there are no cultural barriers for which the land development scheme could not be made successful in some of the centres. In fact, the scheme has been found to be result oriented in the centres where the beneficiaries have voluntarily come forward to derive the benefit. Of course, proper motivation by the concerned department to the beneficiaries is also highly essential since the people have to adopt a new scientific technology. Besides, interviews with a cross-section of the people reveal that the scheme would probably have been more productive if the reclamation of a piece of land was preceded by proper soil testing and a sustained arrangement of irrigation.

Varieties of agricultural seeds, fertilizers, pesticides and tools and implements have been supplied by the concerned department to the people (Table V.13). Similarly, horticultural assistance has also been provided to the people so that they become interested in growing horticultural crops for their economic uplift (Table V.14). According to the beneficiaries they have utilised the seeds of paddy, mustard, sesame and vegetable etc. ; fertilizers and pesticides viz., urea, murate of potash, aldrex, diathene and rogor etc., supplied by the department and in return, they have received satisfactory results. The agricultural implements like spade, sickle, *dao* and plough etc., have also benefitted the people to a great extent. On the other hand, the attitude of the people towards the practice of horticultural crops, mainly cultivation of pineapple is found to be very lukewarm except the people inhabiting the centres of Kekang Adong and Thijoklangso.

These two centres are located within Deothar area which is, in fact, the nerve centre of pineapple cultivation in the district. That is why, the department has also supplied sufficient quantity of pineapple suckers in these two centres. In other centres the people are not found to be taking proper care for luxuriant growth of the pineapple plants. Most of the people are of the opinion that their centres do not have the desired type of soil and land topography to have a profitable pineapple cultivation. However, the beneficiaries of Rongnagar centre have grown arecanut, banana, papaya, pineapple, *litchi* and citrus fruits etc., and have received good returns. On the whole, it seems, the people have given relatively more importance to agricultural input in comparison to horticultural input. However, it may be noted that most of the beneficiaries have not given due follow-up weightage towards application of fertilizers and pesticides in their agricultural as well as horticultural fields after the initiation of the supply of the items by the department. In fact, the department also did not take any follow-up measure to ensure the regular use of the same in their fields. Obviously the yields in subsequent years have gone much below the desired amount. Proper motivation alongwith necessary training to the people is expected to create awareness among them for developing a practice of scientific agriculture. This in turn is likely to keep them away from the age-old shifting cultivation for all time to come.

Bullocks and pigs have been supplied to the people of the selected centres by the Department of Animal Husbandry & Veterinary. Bullocks are used for cultivating the low-lying areas. Pigs are meant for enhancing their economy to the possible extent. Data generated from the field reveal that the people of the centres have been immensely benefitted by the provision of bullocks. In Rongbong Adong centre initially 3 pair of bullocks were distributed. But this provision could hardly solve the problems of the cultivators since they had to carry out agricultural activities with the help of these bullocks on rotation basis. As such, they appealed to the implementing authority to supply more bullocks to the centre. The difficulties experienced by the people in cultivating the land were favourably considered and the department provided the centre with an additional subsidy of 10 more pair of bullocks. As a result of this additional subsidy, the beneficiaries have been reported to have carried out the agricultural operations without any sort of inconvenience. Similarly, the people could, by and large, derive financial benefit from the piggery scheme too. In fact, the provision of bullocks and pigs under the IJDP has positively helped the people to augment their economic condition to a reasonable extent.

Notwithstanding the dearth of suitable land for pisciculture the Department of Fisheries has developed ten community fisheries in seven centres. Besides, fish seeds alongwith slaked lime, raw cowdung, chemical fertilizers like urea, super phosphate and murate of potash, rice bran and mustard oil cakes etc., have been supplied to the fisheries. In Rongnagar centre a community fishery was constructed with financial involvement of Rs. 81,000.00 during 1986-87 by the department. The fishery was provided with 13,000 fish seeds out of which 4,500 and 8,500 fish seeds were given by the department and the people of the centre respectively. In addition, 30 tins of lime and 6 bags of mustard oil cakes were also provided to the fishery. The total amount of production of fish was 23.60 quintals. Out of this total yield, 3.60 quintals were consumed by the village people and the remaining 20 quintals were sold in the market at the rate of Rs.30.00 per kilogram. It may relevantly be noted here that there are also some other community fisheries under the programme. But it has been observed that the people of their own have not made any sincere effort to have largescale commercial production of fish in those fisheries. Whatever small quantity they get is generally shared by the people for domestic consumption only. Nevertheless, a probing investigation in this regard makes it apparent that with proper training, subsidies and motivation, the people by and large are likely to accept scientific pisciculture as one of the sustained means to improve their economic condition. In other words, while exploring the alternative pursuits for the *jhumias* under discussion, pisciculture probably deserves a relatively greater weightage.

The Department of Handloom and Textiles has provided improved looms alongwith accessories and yarn in two IJDP centres. Moreover, provision of C.I. sheets has also been made for construction of loom shed. As reported by the beneficiaries, they have properly utilised the looms and have derived satisfactory benefits. Besides domestic consumption, they could sell their surplus products in the local markets. Most of them could thereby add a satisfactory cash amount to their total family income. Now-a-days, the Karbi textiles made in fusion of traditional and modern designs are in great demand. The different rallies, processions and public meetings organised for the movement of autonomous Karbi Anglong have also made the people always conscious of attiring themselves in exquisite style. As a result of this development the Karbi females most of the time are found to remain engaged in weaving varieties of clothes with artistic designs. Thus, the distribution of improved looms in several IJDP centres would have undoubtedly benefitted the *jhumias* to a greater extent. The Department of Industries has also distributed sewing machines in two centres so that the people may take up tailoring as a subsidiary occupation. According to the beneficiaries they have made use of the machines for augmenting their economy besides making varieties of clothes for their home consumption. Bordoloi (1984 : 32) comments, "Emergence of a class of dynamic entrepreneurs from the tribal societies of Assam is yet a dream. The inertia from which the tribal societies is suffering in this respect is yet to be overcome. In a society where the members produce what they need without any profit motive and where wants are still limited, motivation for entrepreneurship is bound to be lacking. But this does not mean that there are no entrepreneurs among the tribal communities. Some kind of entrepreneurship is always found to be prevalent among them. There are artisans, weavers, handicrafts manufacturers among them which have enabled the societies to survive as self-sufficient units. But what they lack is motivation for commercial purpose. If the entrepreneurship is properly developed, the tribal youths will not only be self-employed but they will be employers as well. When they will be in a position to employ someone they will surely think of their own people."

With regard to the economic development of Assam as a whole, Das (1997 : 4) emphasizes, "Agriculture cannot absorb the entire rural labour force. As such a firm policy on decentralisation of industry with emphasis on cottage industry and rural crafts is highly essential for economic development of the rural people in particular and economically backward people of Assam in general".

The Rubber Plantation scheme is implemented in two centres out of the ten IJDP centres during the period of five years. The names of the centres are Phanglangso and Kaipani. The scheme has been implemented at Phanglangso during 1988-89 covering 20 hectares of land. In Kaipani centre it has been implemented in 5 hectares of land during 1989-90. Production has not yet been started from the plantations. Generally the *jhumias* do not show much interest in rubber cultivation since they have to wait for the long gestation period of six years for getting production of rubber. However, the ten rubber estates under the Assam Plantation Crops Development Corporation (APCDC) in the district of Karbi Anglong have shown encouraging results. Moreover, many individuals have utilised their land for rubber plantation succesfully. In such a situation the people of the centres are likely to come forward to carry out rubber plantation wholeheartedly in the near future.

Another important scheme implemented under the IJDP is the Bamboo Plantation. Out of the ten centres, two centres viz., Langhonjar and Recho Apam have been provided with bamboo plantations. The people of the centres are expected to derive financial benefit by way of selling the products in the nearby Nagaon Paper Mill of the Hindustan Paper Corporation Ltd. The total area of land brought under the plantation is 10 hectares in Langhonjar and 15 hectares in Recho Apam. The bamboo plantations have also been surrounded by necessary fencing. Unfortunately, the scheme could not be made successful due to depredations of wild elephants. Over and above, 11 households out of the total number of 55 households of Recho Apam centre have been compelled to leave the centre for good after one year of implementation of the schemes under the IJDP. They had to leave the area because of their being repeatedly attacked by the wild elephants. Incidentally, it may be mentioned here that these eleven households had been living separately from other households of the centre, and as such were more exposed to elephant attacks.

Notwithstanding some differential observations in the nature and extent of positive impact of the different schemes for various possible reasons, on the whole, it may be admitted that the people of the IJDP centres, by and large, have favourably responded to the efforts of the Government as well as the Karbi Anglong District Council in regulating *jhum*. Of course, it does not necessarily mean that the people have completely given up the practice of *jhuming* as a result of the implementation of the schemes. The study reveals that only 17.07% of the total households in the selected centres are non-*jhumias* i.e. they do not carry out *jhuming* operations. And, 11.26% of the total households have been found to be solely engaged in *jhuming* (cf. Table V.11). On the other hand, the percentage of households carrying out *jhum* partially is 71.67. Individual and group interviews carried out in a cross section of the beneficiaries during the present investigation make it apparent that most of the people have realised the gravity of the situation arising out of the practice of shifting cultivation. Consequently, they have now been putting more emphasis on settled cultivation and other alternative means. But however, they carry out *jhuming* partially to supplement their livelihood. In this context it may not be out of place to emphasize here that the IJDP is the first co-ordinated approach of the Government departments for weaning the *jhumias* away from the harmful practice of shifting cultivation. It is, therefore, quite natural that the people from a tradition bound community like the hill Karbis cannot be expected to give up *jhuming* completely within the stipulated time frame. This is mainly because of the fact that many of their socio-cultural and religious customs and practices are intimately associated with the age-old shifting cultivation. But it is reassuring to note that due to the implementation of the schemes the overall attitude of the people towards shifting cultivation has considerably changed. Now-a-days, like their forefathers, they do not completely depend on *jhuming,* but however, they do it partially for their sustenance. This is indeed a significant achievement so far as the *jhum* control programme i.e. the *Integrated Jhumia Development Programme* is concerned.

In order to have a deeper probe to gain some further insight into the attitude and behaviour pattern of the *jhumias* towards the *jhum* control schemes under the IJDP, some concrete cases have been collected from a number of informants representing different centres. A few selected ones are reproduced in the following pages.

> ***Case No. 1.*** *Mr. Sarsing Timung, aged 37 years is an inhabitant of Rongnagar centre and an L.P. school teacher by profession. After passing the Pre University level examination, he discontinued his studies. Mr. Timung's religion is Hinduism. He is the secretary of the village level development committee of the IJDP. In 1987, i.e. at the time of execution of the programme his family consisted of five members. Besides his wife he had three children–one daughter and two sons. The girl was then reading in the primary school. At present, he has two more daughters. All the children are now reading in Primary and High School standards.*
>
> *A detailed interview was arranged with him on 24 April, 1993 at his home to have an idea about his own attitude etc., towards the IJDP and the relevant facts.*
>
> *Although agriculture is the secondary occupation of Mr. Timung, he is very much interested in agricultural activities. Before implementation of the IJDP schemes he himself carried out jhuming in 3 bighas of land every year. He did this in addition to the wet paddy cultivation. When the various schemes under the IJDP were launched in the centre he gave up jhuming completely. Moreover, as*

a Secretary he tried to persuade the people of the centre to make the implementation of the welfare schemes a grand success and to wean them away from the shifting cultivation. Ultimately he came out successful in his endeavour to a reasonable degree.

According to Mr. Timung the IJDP has taught the people of the centre how gardening can be done in a small plot of land with bamboo fencing in and around their homesteads. The people did not make any such attempt before implementation of the scheme. Pineapple suckers, litchi, arecanut and papaya etc., supplied to them under the IJDP have been planted and encouraging results have been achieved. In other words, the latent potentialities of the people have been brought to the surface through the IJDP. However, he states that initially there were some drawbacks. For example, supply of agricultural inputs from the concerned department was irregular and some of the agricultural tools and implements were of low standard. Moreover, the people did not invest sufficient labour as they ought to do. With time the things have changed. Most of the people have now realised that without hard work nobody can prosper in the present age. It is a positive sign that many of them are, at present, in a position to preserve necessary seeds for their future use also. Mr. Timung mentions that the Agriculture Department has supplied various agricultural inputs such as seeds, seedlings, fertilizers and pesticides etc., and has asked the people to distribute the same among themselves. This implies that the property now belongs to the people themselves and it is upto them to make proper use of these. This has generated great enthusiasm among the people and they have, in fact, distributed the inputs equally. Mr. Timung states that he has himself cultivated HYV seeds viz., IR-8 and Pankaj in his agricultural fields and has received around 6 quintals of paddy per bigha.

So far as the distribution of bullocks by the Department of Animal Husbandry and Veterinary is concerned, it is reported by him that 10 pair of bullocks have been supplied by the department during the year 1990-91 to the centre. It is heartening to note that the whole centre consisting of 72 households is divided into 10 strata, comprising 7 households in each stratum. The remaining 2 households are given Rs.700.00 each against non-provision of bullocks. On the whole, the people have been greatly benefitted by the provision of bullocks.

The spirit of co-operation which is already in existence among the people have been futher strengthened by the schemes implemented under the IJDP. The community fishery constructed by the Department of fisheries in the centre is indeed a commendable work. The people have actively participated in the production of fish. Besides consumption of fish, the people have also sold the yields in the market. Moreover, he states that they have done mustard cultivation in a plot of land measuring about 48 bighas on co-operative basis and they have received good returns at the rate of 3 quintals per bigha. Necessary seeds and fertilizers have been supplied to them by the concerned department through the IJDP.

On the contrary, Mr. Timung regrets that the Department of Irrigation has not performed its activities upto the desired level. The department asked the people to clear the jungle on the land proposed for minor irrigation. Accordingly the people completed the job of jungle clearing. But unfortunately no further step was taken by the department to irrigate the agricultural lands.

On the whole, Mr. Timung says that the overall impact of the jhum control schemes under IJDP on the people inhabiting Rongnagar centre is satisfactory. He earnestly hopes that more people of the centre will give up jhuming completely in the near future. Moreover, he proudly says that even at this stage Rongnagar centre is far more advanced in all spheres in comparison to other neighbouring Karbi villages.

Case No. 2. *Mr. Langtuk Teron, an inhabitant of Tikaklangso centre is 56 years old. He is a cultivator and has read upto primary standard. A Hindu by religion, Mr. Teron heads a nuclear family consisting of five inmates. The other members, besides him are his wife (50 years), two daughters (20 and 16 years respectively) and a son (18 years). The children and their mother are all illiterate.*

He was interviewed on 28 November, 1993 at his home. Before implementation of the IJDP in the centre he did not have any wet paddy cultivation. He had to depend solely on 8 bighas of jhum land for the maintenance of the family. In addition to jhum lands he had 2 bighas of land under horticulture and also 2 more bighas of land under homestead. He possessed 12 bighas of land altogether. From the jhum fields in a year he received about 16 quintals of paddy, 3 quintals of maize, 2 quintals of sesame and some amount of vegetables like arum, chilli and gourd etc. The total value of the production was around Rs. 5,500.00. Moreover, he received an approximate amount of Rs.1,000.00 from horticultural crops viz., pineapple, banana and betel nut etc. In addition, Mr. Teron obtained around Rs.1,500.00 and Rs. 2,000.00 from poultry and piggery respectively. On the whole, the approximate annual income in the year just before implementation of the schemes was to the tune of Rs.10,000.00.

After implemention of the Land Development scheme in the centre he reduced jhuming activities and confined the same only in 3 bighas of land. On the other hand, he got 8 bighas of land reclaimed under the IJDP. However, out of 8 bighas, only 4 bighas were provided with irrigation facilities. In this context he reports that only two minor irrigation dams have been constructed under this programme in the centre to provide benefits to ten households by each dam.

Mr. Teron says that under the IJDP 12 pair of bullocks were supplied to the centre by the Department of Animal Husbandry and Veterinary during 1990-91. He received one pair of bullocks for carrying out agricultural activities. This has benefitted him a lot in carrying out the agricultural activities as well as in getting a better yield. On enquiry about the continuation of jhum he says that he practises it partially although he receives low yield in comparison to wet paddy cultivation. His children do not go to school and they extend helping hands in carrying out jhum. He grows mixed crops in the jhum fields and as a result, he gets varieties of products in addition to paddy. Moreover, he says that jhum rice is relatively more tasteful. However, he opines that if irrigation facilities are available in other 4 bighas of land under his possession, he will give up jhuming completely.

He states that there is no other alternative to jhum for the people of the centre since well developed lands with proper irrigation facilities are lacking. The location of the centre in between the two ranges of hills also stands in the way of getting suitable lands for wet cultivation. Moreover, the number of schemes implemented under the IJDP is limited as a result of which only few households including himself have been able to derive benefits out of the schemes. He lays more emphasis on the implementation of the schemes relating to cottage and small scale industries lie weaving, bamboo and cane works, carpentry, bee-keeping and tailoring etc.

Case No. 3. *Mr. Rensing Teron is an inhabitant of Kekang Adong centre. A Christian by religion, Mr. Teron (35 years) is a young promising contractor. He heads a nuclear family having his wife and two sons (7 and 5 years) as inmates. He was interviewed on 10 September, 1994 at his home.*

The total area of land possessed by Mr. Teron before the implementation of the welfare schemes under the IJDP is 31 bighas. Out of this jhum and wet lands cover 15 bighas and 10 bighas respectively. Horticultural land consists of 4 bighas while homestead land comprises 2 bighas. After implementation of the schemes in the centre he has given up jhuming completely and engaged himself in the production of horticultural crops viz., pineapple, banana and citrus etc., and wet paddy cultivation.

Like other people of the centre Mr. Teron has received various agricultural inputs such as ginger, pineapple suckers and citrus etc., through the IJDP. The agricultural implements received by him are hoe, rake, fork and spade etc. He has also received one piggery unit in 1987, one sewing machine in 1988 and one pair of bullocks in 1991. According to him he has achieved success by means of utilising the aforesaid items. He has also undergone a three-day training in the year 1991 organised for imparting knowledge to the people about plantation and manuring of citrus. At present, he receives around Rs.10,000.00 per annum by way of selling pineapple and citrus.

Mr. Teron states that a community fishery was constructed under the IJDP during 1987-88. But no steps are taken till now for sale of the products. However, fishes are sometimes caught and distributed among the households of the centre for consumption.

According to Mr. Teron the total area of land under jhum is more than that of wet cultivation in the centre. Efforts are being channelised mainly to engage the people of the centre in horticultural activities through supply of varieties of horticultural crops free of cost under the IJDP and to help the people wean away from jhum. But the people cannot depend mainly on these crops grown in limited areas due to several factors such as low yield, fluctuation of market price and communication bottleneck in the disposal of the perishable products etc. That is why, they carry out jhuming. Of course, it is encouraging to note that after implementation of the schemes most of the people in the centre practise jhuming partially only. Mr. Teron further comments that inspite of the difficulties Kekang Adong cente may still be considered as one of the advanced IJDP centres in the district.

When asked about the possibilities of exploring means of regulating jhum in Karbi Anglong he engrossed himself in deep thoughts for a while and replied that a number of suitable schemes pursued for about 3-4 years followed by constant monitoring will help control jhuming in future. The major hiatus in the IJDP, according to him is that there is no proper follow up action. Schemes have been implemented with huge financial involvement but no concrete steps have been taken to know whether the schemes as a whole have vehemently jerked the nerves of the common mass for keeping them away from shifting cultivation or not. Perhaps lack of proper motivation, lack of follow up action, low level of literacy and go-easy life of the people etc., are the primary factors responsible for continuation of such a primitive method of agriculture even in a Christian dominated centre like Kekang Adong--Mr. Teron concludes.

On the whole, it may be said that the people of the centres have been putting all possible efforts to have an amicable negotiation with the changing situations and thereby gradually adapting to present-day needs. They have accepted new technology of production for their overall development in complete harmony with their traditional social organisation. No apparent adverse effect on their cultural values has been observed due to the introduction of various welfare schemes. A few decades back the *jhumias* could not think of giving up the age-old shifting cultivation and adopting new methods of cultivation. Now-a-days, they are gradually getting habituated with settled mode of cultivation. Similar observations have been made by some other scholars also in the context of some other society. Thus, for example, in connection with a study on the Dimasa, a major tribe in the North Cachar Hills district of Assam, Bora (1992 : 103) maintains, "The findings from the study of the Dimasa situation indicate that there is no reason to believe that there would be maladjustment in the socio-economic life, if a tribe practising *jhum* cultivation is taken to sedentary cultivation. So, the theories that '*jhuming* is a way of life and the tribe does not like to leave it' and that 'the tribals are conservative and they do not like to accept alternative way of earning' appear to be no longer tenable"

VII

SUMMARY AND CONCLUSION

The chapter has been devoted to recapitulate and summarise the data presented and discussed in the preceding chapters. In the process some concluding remarks have also been incorporated here and there. An endeavour has been made to highlight the salient features of the *Integrated Jhumia Development Programme* (IJDP) implemented in the two autonomous hill districts of Karbi Anglong and North Cachar Hills in Assam and to assess the impact of the *jhum* control programme on the Karbis inhabiting the district of Karbi Anglong.

The research project, "Impact of the Integrated Jhumia Development Programme on the Hill Tribes of Assam : A Case Study among the Karbis" was conducted in 10 selected centres in Karbi Anglong to attempt an objective assessment and understanding of the impact of the different schemes under the programme on the Karbis.

The broad objectives of the study were as follows:

(i) To have a detailed idea of the different schemes under the programme as well as their mode of implementation in the centres.

(ii) To have an assessment of the prevailing state of affairs with regard to the co-ordination between the potential beneficiaries and the implementing agency/personnel.

(iii) People's attitude towards the age-old practice of shifting cultivation vis-a-vis the alternative permanent mode of livelihood.

(iv) To have an idea about the difference/s (if any) in the extent of *jhum* cultivation before and after the implementation of the programme.

(v) Beneficiaries' views with regard to their overall economic condition before and after implementation of the programme.

(vi) To have an overall assesment of the impact of the programme on the life of the Karbis.

The hypothesis, "The IJDP has taken care of all the relevant aspects and is being accepted by the people without leading to a social disorganisation" has, in fact, two prongs, namely; (i) The IJDP has taken care of all the relevant aspects, and (ii) The IJDP is being accepted by the people without leading to a social disorganisation.

To generate the mass of data embodied in the dissertation, standard anthropological methods and techniques have been used during the field work that has been carried out between April, 1993 and January, 1995. Various tools e.g. Interview schedules, open ended interview (individual and group), observation and collection of concrete cases etc., have been used either independently or in collaboration depending on the nature of data needed to be collected. Important particulars in relation to each centre viz., location, transport and communication system, civic and educational facilities and other basic amenities have been collected independently in a separate schedule. It may, however, be noted here that while collecting field data emphasis has always been put more on qualitative aspects.

Assam, since prehistoric period has been the adobe of various tribal communities with diverse origins and cultures. According to the Scheduled Castes and Scheduled Tribes (Amendment) Act, 1976 fourteen tribes have been specified in the autonomous hill districts while nine tribes have been specified in the plains districts of Assam. The Karbi Anglong district is located between latittudes 25°30′ and 26°41′ N and longitudes 92°7 and 93°52′E while the North Cachar Hills district is located between latitudes 25° and 25°45′ N and longitudes 92°30′E. The two districts are marked by hill ranges with meandering rivers and fertile river valleys. According to 1991 Census the Karbi Anglong district covers 13.3% and 2.95% of the total geographical area and total population of Assam respectively. On the other hand, the North Cachar Hills district covers 6.2% and 0.67% of the total geographical area and total population of the State respectively.

As per provisions of the Sixth Schedule to the constitution of India, the North Cachar Hills District Council and the Karbi Anglong (Mikir Hills) District Council have come into existence on 20th April and 23rd

June, 1952 respectively. The civil subdivisions of Karbi Anglong are Diphu, Hamren and Bokajan while those of North Cachar Hills are Haflong and Maibang.

According to 1991 Census the total scheduled tribe population in Karbi Anglong constitutes 51.56% of the total population of the district. Similary, in North Cachar Hills it accounts for 65.54% of the total population of the district. Although many tribes inhabit the two districts the predominant tribes are the Karbis in Karbi Anglong and the Dimasa Kacharis in North Cachar Hills. As per 1971 Census the Karbis constitute 82.29% of the total scheduled tribe population of Karbi Anglong while the Dimasa Kacharis constitute 46.68% of the total scheduled tribe population of North Cachar Hills.

Shifting cultivation which is a primitive method of agriculture is still in existence across the globe and is known by different nomenclatures. In North-eastern India it is also known by different local terms but it is commonly referred to as *jhum* and the cultivators are known as the *jhumias*. It has been noted that the precise data on the extent of shifting cultivation in the world are not available. However, the F.A.O. has estimated it to be about 36 million sq km in the world. Again, various authorities have provided with various estimates at different times in relation to the total area of land under shifitng cultivation and the total tribal population involved in it in India. The Task Force Report (1983) reveals that among the North-eastern States the annual area under shifting cultivation is the highest in Manipur and the lowest in Nagaland. The fallow period varies from 2 to 10 years in this region. It is indeed a difficult task to know whether the shifting cultivation is increasing or decreasing in India Kar (1986 : 41) observes that the total area of land under shifting cultivation and the population dependent on it have increased in all the States of North-east India and Orissa while in other States the shifting cultivation has shown a decreasing trend or a total elimination. Various authorities indicate that the population sustaining capacity of land under shifting cultivation is very low. It varies from 3 to 16 persons per sq km.

In by gone days the duration of *jhum* cycles were significantly longer since the density of population was low. At present, the population has increased manifold and the *jhum* cycles have considerably shortened. The land cannot recuperate the lost fertility and therefore, the production decreases. In short, the land-man ratio is badly affected. Consequently, the shifting cultivation leads to heavy soil erosion, loss of forests and an overall imbalance in the eco-system.

Under shifting cultivation the traditional pattern of land ownership is community oriented. The cultivator has the usufractuary right over the *jhum* land which he cultivates for a short duration. In fact, the economic activities are performed with the full involvement of most of the people belonging to the community. Besides, various socio-religious practices are intertwined with the different phases of shifting cultivation.

In Karbi Anglong district the approximate ratio of hills to plains is 60 : 40. The hill area covers State Reserved Forests, District Council Reserved Forests and the Unclassified Forests. The Unclassified Forests include hills and low-lying forest lands. The people varry out *jhuming* in the hills while they practise other cultivations in the low-lying forest lands after reclamation. The people consider themselves to be the common owners of the hills and the Karbi Anglong District Council doed not generally oppose to the system of common ownership. According to the Report of the National Commission on Agriculture (1976) the total area of land affected by *jhum* in Karbi Anglong and North Cachar Hills is 4,15,000 hectares and 83,000 hectares respectively. The tribal families involved in it are 45,000 in Karbi Anglong and 13,000 in North Cachar Hills. Again, the Assam Remote Sensing Application Centre reveals that in the recent years *jhuming* has increased in the two hill districts of Assam. In Karbi Anglong, the area under current *jhum* has increased from 13,583 hectares in 1986-87 to 69,125 hectares in 1993-94. Similarly, in North Cachar Hills it has increased from 22,807 hectares in 1986-87 to 69,447 hectares in 1993-94. The total area affected by *jhum* has increased from 56.95% to 60.10% in Karbi Anglong and from 46.51% to 56.18% in North Cachar Hills.

Studies on different aspects of shifting cultivation have been undertaken by various authorities. In North-east India, the Agro-Economic Research Centre, Jorhat; the NEC, Shillong; the ICAR, Shillong; and various individual social scientists have carried out a good number of studies. Most of the studies reveal that the shifting cultivation leads to soil erosion and destruction of forests. Over and above, output per acre and output per worker are very low in this system of cultivation. That is why, the system is not suitable for economic change and development. In all the studies suggestions have invariably been made to explore alternative and sustainable means of livelihood so that the people, in the long run can do away with this primitive practice.

In order to regulate te practice of shifting cultivation the Mikir Hills District (*Jhuming)* Regulation, 1954 was passed by the District Council. The Executive Committee of the District Council was vested with all powers in relation to the regulation of *jhuming* in the district. This Regulation curtailed the powers of the Village Councils to select *jhum* sites and to distribute the same among the families according to their needs. This had generated much resentment among the people. As a result, the regulation was amended in the year 1966. The amendment made the provision of selecting *jhum* sites by the people in consultation with *Sarkari Gaonbura* and local *Mouzadar*. However, on any disagreement, the two functionaries would refer the matter to the Executive Committee for final decision.

As a part of *jhum* control measure, the Development Departments have also executed several schemes in the two hill districts of Assam and these have been discussed in details in *Chapter Two*. As noted earlier, in the present study, an effort has been made to have some evaluation of the different schemes in terms of the proposed targets and actual realisation of the same. In most of the cases there have been gaps that can be explained in terms of the observable flaws and gaps in the modus operandi. In the Karbi Anglong district 10 model villages were established in 1960s. But many families went again to their original habitat leaving the model villages due to lack of follow-up action of the programme, lack of motivation to stay in the model villages, non-repairing of the houses despite abundant raw materials and non-construction of traditional type of Karbi houses etc. In order to motivate the *jhumias* towards plantation crops, the Assam Plantation Crops Development Corporation (APCDC) was created in 1974. Both coffee and rubber estates have shown encouraging results. But the plantations after maturity have to be transferred to the *jhumia* beneficiaries @ one hectare per family. However, complete transfer of the plantations has not yet taken place.

The Planning Commission introduced Composite Project from 1974-75 under Special Central Assistance for inducing the *jhumias* towards settled cultivation as well as protection of forest cover in the two hill districts of Assam. The scheme was, however, unsuccessful mainly due to lack of proper co-ordination between the concerned departments. As a result, the Planning Commission decided to replace it by the *Integrated Jhumia Development Programme* (IJDP). Initially 10 experimental centres under this programme were taken up for a period of 5 years from 1982-83 and the results were satisfactory in comparison to that of the Composite Projects. Being encouraged with the results of the experimental centres, the Government took up 34 IJDP centres with a total population of 2,157 households in the two hill districts of Assam for a period of 5 years from 1986-87 to 1990-91.

Again, in the year 1989, under the Central Sector *Jhum* Control Programme, two Compact Areas viz., Chinthong and Hadingma have been identified and various schemes have been implemented for a period of three years. Like Compact Area approach, four Mini Compact Areas viz., Hidipi, Miyungdisa, Digerkuki and Jinam Valley have been identified under State Sector *Jhum* Control Programme and the schemes have been implemented for a period of four years from 1991-92. Thus, it has been found that a good number of programmes have been launched in the two hill districts of Assam to control *jhuming*. Some of the schemes have proved successful while some others have met with failures.

In view of the fact that the intensive investigation has been carried out among the people belonging to a particular ethnic group, the discourse relevantly includes a chapter (No.III) that provides a brief ethnographic note on the Karbis highlighting various aspects viz., their origin and migration, socio-economic and religious organisation, traditional pattern of administration and traditional institutions etc. Ethnically the Karbis belong to the great Mongoloid group and linguistically they belong to the Tibeto-Burman branch of the Sino-Tibetan group. Their exáct affinity with other tribes has not been properly determined. Grierson classifies them between the Bodo and the Western Naga. On the other hand, Lyall attempts to classify them with the tribes that provide the connecting link between the Nagas and the Kuki-Chins, particularly the latter. The ballads prevalent among the Karbis also refer to their close relation with the Kuki-Chins.

The original habitat of the Karbis is supposed to be the Western China from where they migrated to Burma. Later on, they entered into Assam through the North-eastern route. In the initial stage they could not live happily in one place. They had to move from place to place mainly due to attacks by the Kachari and the Jayantia kings and the Burmese invaders. At last they made their settlements in Karbi Anglong in large proportion.

As a result of their contact with the surrounding tribes they acquired many cultural elements from those tribes.

The Karbis have five exogamous clans viz., *Teron, Inghi, Ingti, Terang* and *Timung*. Teron (1974 : 7) mentions that Teron, *Inghi, Ingti, Terang* and *Timung* clans have been divided into 6, 30, 5, 6 and 30 sub-clans respectively. Monogamy is the prevailling practice among the people. Marriage by negotiation is the common practice followed by them. They have a patriarchal family system. Descent is traced through the male line. The nuclear family is predominant in comparison to the joint family.

The Karbi villages are generally small in size. The village is normally known by the name of the headman of the particular village. Although the people establish their villages on the hill slopes, many villages are also seen in the plains areas. The traditional housing pattern is pile dwelling. Now-a-days, houses are constructed on grounds also. An idea about the household tools and implements usually possessed by a Karbi family can be had from the materials presented in *Chapter Three (The Karbis)*.

Agriculture is the main source of livelihood of the people. They carry out both *jhum* and wet cultivation. Cattle, pigs and poultry are also reared by them. The people are expert in bamboo and cane products which are mainly used for household consumption. They are economically not very sound and therefore, are acutely affected by land alienation and indebtedness. Das (1987 : 181) reports that in a study of over 200 families, 80% of the Karbis have been found to be the victims of *paikas* system of mortgaging and indebtedness.

The staple diet of the people is rice with vegetables, edible roots and tubers etc. Pork, chicken and fish are their delicacies. They like to drink tea without milk and sugar. Their favourite beverage is rice beer. The Karbis have their traditional dress and ornaments. However, the use of the traditional articles has been gradually decreasing particularly among the younger generation.

So far as religion is concerned, Hinduism has exerted great influence among them. Of course, traditional beliefs and practices are also prevalent. They believe in the Supreme God (Arnam Kethe). Besides, they worship a good number of benevolent and malevolent deities also. They have no idol, temple or shrine. They do not worship trees and animals. *Chojun* is an important household religious festival among them. But *Chomangkan* i.e. shraddha ceremony is the most important and expensive religious festival of the Karbis. It may be noted here that a section of the people has also been influenced by Christianity.

The traditional mode of administration among the Karbis represents a three-tier system – the *Lindokpo* at the top, the Habes at the middle and the *Sarthes* at the grass root level. Although this type of administration is, at present, obsolete, the Karbi *Recho* (King) still plays a vital role in the socio-religious life of the people of Hamren subdivision in the district of Karbi Anglong.

In every Karbi village there is a village council *(Me)* which comprises all the adult members of the village as members (*Chakri)* and the headman *(Sarthe)* as the President. The bachelor's dormitory known as Terang, Farla or Jirkedam among the people has of late gradually disappeared. The institution of youth club *(Risomar)* is, however, observed among them, particularly in east Karbi Anglong. Grain bank *(Kerung Amei)* is also an important traditional institution which is still in vogue among the people.

While dealing with the basic infrastructural facilities and population characteristics *(cf. Chapter Four)* it has been observed that the people are not in a position to derive sufficient benefit out of road communication facilities. This is mainly because of their distant location. Five centres fall in the range of around 4 km while four centres fall in the range of 5-9 km from the nearest motorable road. Moreover, one centre is located at a distance of 25 km from the motorable road. The locational problem in terms of distance without having any alternative means of transport and communication seems to have stood in the way of deriving the desired amount of benefit from a number of other establishments also. Thus, for example, despite the presence of railway services, Development Blocks, Post and Telegraph facilities, modern medi-care centres and the educational institutions, the people do not seem to have been taking the optimum services. Although the primary schools have been established in all the centres, the literacy rate among the people is around 32%. Besides, the students' strength in post-primary level generally goes down very sharply. The present study reveals that out of the ten centres, 7 centres do not have a single individual who has passed the High School Leaving Certificate Examination (erstwhile Matriculation Examination). The remaining 3 centres viz., Rongnagar, Kekang Adong and Thijoklangso have altogether 17 individuals (12 males and 5 females) having the qualification in the category 'H.S.L.C. & Above' (cf. Table IV.8). Thus, the state of affairs with regard to education among the people of the centres does not seem to be very encouraging. Unless some steps are taken to bring about a substantial change in the field of education by establishing sufficient number of shcools with provisions of necessary paraphernalia and by motivating the guardians to send their wards to the schools, it will not be possible to eradicate illiteracy and achieve an effective socio-economic change among the people. Further, while framing the school curriculum, a course may be included to highlight the harmful effects of shifting cultivation. This education in the school level supported by identical efforts by some other agencies through audio-visual aids or other means is expected to create a relatively more favourable atmosphere for adopting some permanent source of livelihood by the people.

While dwelling more on the education scenario, it may be noted that a recent survey report (1997 : 58) on the 'Status of Primary Education in Karbi Anglong District' conducted by the Assam Institute of Research for Tribals and Scheduled Castes, Guwahati through the District Research Office, Diphu reveals, "Although there is high enrolment in the early stage i.e. Class I, the momentum is not maintained in the upper classes. Thus, in Class IV there is sharp fall in the enrolment due to various socio-economic and infrastructural factors. Therefore, the increased enrolment cannot be the criterion for an upward trend of educational standard. There is no academic environment in the villages. Facilities like chair and table are not available and the parents are also not in a position to supply the same. Besides, the parents are so busy in outdoor activities that they do not get any time to keep their sons and daughters busy in study. Furthermore, the parents utilise the services of their sons and daughters in household activities. The parents should spare the children from household activities".

The daily and weekly markets play an important role in the socio-economic life of the people. In the market the people sell their agricultural products and in return, they purchase their daily necessities. Moreover, it is the meeting place of various sections of people representing different walks of life. So far as the studied centres are concerned, most of the people cannot derive these benefits properly since the location of most of the centres is not negotiable with reference to that of the market.

The establishment of Large Area Multipurpose Co-operative Societies (LAMPS) in and around the centres is one of the main objectives of the IJDP. But in reality this has not been materialised. Except three other LAMPS others are located at a distance of around 7 km and above from the centres. As such, the services rendered by the LAMPS to the people cannot probably be considered to be satisfactory. As a matter of fact, the services of the LAMPS numbering 31, at present, in the district of Karbi Anglong are not found to be satisfactory as a whole. Most of them are incurring losses. The main reasons for the same are high transportation cost, shortage of stock, high establishment cost, non-committed staff, marginal profits on essential commodities and huge amount of interest accrued on Government loan etc. Saikia (1984 : 58) comments, "Malpractices, whether consisting of misappropriation or shortage in stocks are not healthy signs for the growth of co-operative ventures and if these unfortunate state of affairs are allowed to go on, the very survival of the societies will be in zeopardy. Constant supervision by the officials of the Co-operative Department may go a long way in checking malpractices amongst the delinquent staff. In this sphere the responsibilities entrusted to the Managing Committee members are also no less important. The system of audit and constant verification will have to be intensified with surprise checks from District Administration".

Banks are also not within easy reach of the people except those of 3 centres which are located within 5 km from the institutions. However, it may be noted here that the people, by and large, consider the prevailing procedures involved in availing bank assistance as very cumbersome. As such, they express reluctance in undertaking this exercise.

On the whole, it may be said that relatively easy accessibility to the basic infrastructural facilities like educational institutions, health institutions, post offices, banks, markets and motorable roads etc., definitely help grow consciusness among the people. The more interior the location of the centres, there appears to be the less possibilities of having basic infrastructural facilities. As a result, the people cannot have the chance of interacting with the people of the outside world. They have to stay in confinement within a specific geographical setting. Recho Apam and Langhonjar are such IJDP centres. Naturally, the level of achievement out of the schemes implemented under the IJDP in these centres is less in comparison to Rongnagar centre. In such a situation the success of the schemes will primarily depend on the efficiency and sincere attitude of the implementing autorities. Sachan (1990 : 166) maintains, "In the absence of trained manpower from among the tribals, most of the people serving in various Government departments in the tribal areas are non-tribals from outside the district. For a long time the tribals were treated as uncivilised by the non-tribals and therefore, sometimes attempts were made to civilise the tribals in such a way that there is a complete change in the pattern of their behaviour and way of life. Many times it is done with good intention and without foreseeing whether this will lead to a cultural conflict and agony for the tribals. Nothing gives rise to so much anger, hostility and even hatres as the apprehension of cultural aggression. It is this apprehension which has been allowed to grow and has given rise to so many problems. It has become a fashion to argue that the tribal people are so ungrateful that even after so much of economic investment on them, they are not satisfied and do not feel obliged to the rest of the world. Economic investment is not a wholesome solution though it may foster understanding. More important, however, is gaining confidence and goodwill of the tribalfolk. Tribal people will have to be convinced through right actions that their culture and way of life will be determined by themselves. It is this lack of sensitivity that many schemes have failed at the level of implementation even though they were planned and conceived well. With more failures the apprehensions grow and add to the problems. Working condition is no doubt harder and it requires special efforts on the part of an officer to make himself acceptable to people at large. It is worthwhile selecting right set of people for serving in tribal areas. From the beginning of the career these officers should be imparted special training, where they are made to understand the culture and ethos of the tribal people". It is, therefore, highly essential to think of the development of the tribal people through the formulation of the welfare schemes to be executed by a band of well-trained and committed personnel.

The total population of the studied centres is 2,865 that is distributed in 533 households. Thus, the average size of a household stands at 5.3. Majority of the families (76.18%), however, has 5 to 6 members. The men-women ratio is 1000 : 930.

That, agriculture is their main source of livelihood is revealed by the fact that around 98% of the families have cultivation as the primary occupation. Some people, however, have taken up other means of livelihood like business, salaried jobs and wage earning.

The total area of land possessed by 533 households is 8,821 *bighas* which include 31.44%, 37.22% of *jhum,* wet and terrace land respectively. The *jhum* lands provide a relatively lesser amount of yield as compared to settled and terrace cultivation. The average landholding per family is 16.5 *bighas* whereas that per capita stands at 3.1 *bighas.* Among the livestock population the pigs and poultry are found in large proportion in the centres. Besides domestic consumption they also sacrifice the animals and birds to appease various deities. However, scientific rearing for commercial purpose has not been observed among them.

The average annual income of a family from all sources has been found to be Rs.13,739.00 against the average annual expenditure of Rs.12,943.00. As such, the average family has a marginal surplus budget of Rs.796.00 only per annum. It, therefore, appears that the people are more or less living in a subsistence level economy.

In the centres various schemes under the IJDP have been implemented for motivating the people towards acceptance of settled mode of livelihood in lieu of practising *jhum.* Most of the schemes though not implemented uniformly in all the centres, seem to have been able to generate favourable response from the *jhumias.* Although many of the beneficiaries have not derived benefits according to their expectations, they have expressed the view that the practice of shifting cultivation should come to an end. However, in the same breath they like to emphasize that they cannot totally discontinue *jhuming* unless some alternative and sustainable permanent ways of earning livelihood are fully ascertained. Perhaps duc to this reason the number of households practising *jhum* partially is found to be as high as 71.67% (cf. Table V.11). Majumdar (1982 : 137) opines, "It is interesting fact that even in the areas where they have opened up land for permanent cultivation, shifting cultivation has persisted as a subsidiary method of cultivation for the following reasons:

(i) A number of traditional vegetables can be grown in shifting cultivation, while utilising every inch of the permanent land for major crops like paddy and millet.

(ii) Some crops like ginger, cotton, hill jute etc., are grown only in the plots of shifting cultivation and such crops give them a steady source of cash income.

(iii) As labour in the shifting plots is supplied both by males and females (rather, in some respects females work more) while in settled agriculture most of the work is done by males. Women's labour can be fruitfully utilized if shifting cultivation is practised side by side with settled agriculture".

According to the beneficiaries there are some flaws so far as the implementation of the schemes are concerned. The land development scheme has been implemented under the programme but irrigation facilities have not been provided adequately. As a result, they have not derived the desired benefits. Sometimes agricultural inputs such as paddy, maize and sesame etc., do not reach the centres in right time and very often the quantity of the inputs is not according to the needs of the beneficiaries. Some of the agricultural tools and implements supplied to the centres are of inferior quality. Bullocks and pigs supplied through the schemes are inadequate in number. Similarly, fly shuttle looms and sewing machines are also insufficient in quantity. In lighter veins the people comment that the schemes meant for the welfare of the people have not been properly implemented although huge amount of money has been spent during the period of five years. This fact, however, cannot be denied that a lot of money has been spent without achieving proportionate results in the IJDP centres. Factors responsible for such a situation may be mainly attributed to the apparent indifferent attitude of some of the implementing authorities and/or the beneficiaries of the centres. It thus seems obvious that the implementing authorities should not only provide the people with adequate assistance in right time but also should motivate and persuade them properly to accept and utilise the assistance for their benefits. On the other hand, the beneficiaries also need to think of utilising the assistance in the best possible manner so that they are in a position to earn their livelihood without resorting to shifting cultivation. In this respect Bhowmick's observations (1990 : 74) are very relevant, "The people for whom the project is going to be implemented should be taken into confidence as to how far this will improve their lot. Recurring assistance in the form of spoon feeding should be discarded. Attempt should be made in such a way that the people can stand on their own feet and realise the endeavour of the government or the voluntary organizations. It is true that the problem cannot be removed within a short time".

As a matter of fact, the present study reveals that some selected people of some selected centres, who of their own are very much aware of the positive implications of the new ideas and technologies have derived maximum benefits out of the schemes under the IJDP. Rongnagar centre is probably an ideal example in this case. People are highly conscious. They are sincere and hard working. They have learnt the method of gardening through the IJDP. A visit to the centre will make any one thrilled with joy to see the betel nut, *litchi* and other plants near their homesteads. They have also shown that pisciculture may be undertaken on community basis. They have earned good amount of cash by selling fish products from the community fishery constructed under the IJDP.

As noted earlier, it has been observed that the schemes under the IJDP have not been implemented equally in all the centres. The number of schemes varies from centre to centre. Moreover, continuous assistance to the people has not been provided for the whole period of five years. As a result, the actual spirit of the people towards adoption of settled mode of livelihood has not been elevated to the desired extent. Thus, it seems, instead of taking up as many as 17 centres at a time in the district, selection of limited centres and implementation of a good number of ambitious schemes for a period of 3 to 4 years without any interruption alongwith proper motivation and constant monitoring with a missionary zeal would in all probability have brought greater achievement in *jhum* control.

Notwithstanding these shortcomings, the present study, however, reveals that as the first co-ordinated approach the *Integrated Jhumia Development Programme* (IJDP) has succeeded in awakening the hill Karbis against the harmful effects or *jhuming* and taking up alternative mode of livelihood to a certain extent. The programme does not seem to have any observable counterproductive impact on the traditional socio-religious and political institutions of the people. Thus, on the basis of the data generated from the field, it seems, the second part of the proposed hypothesis, "The IJDP is being accepted by the people without leading to a social disorganisation" is acceptable. But, the first, part, "The IJDP has taken care of all the relevant aspects" has not been found to be valid.

Suggestions

Before concluding the discussion, it may not be out of place here to incorporate a few relevant observations/suggestions/recommendations for being considered by the appropriate authorities in the formulation and implementation of the *jhum* control programmes for the tribal people in general and those of Karbi Anglong in particular.

1. The selection of the centres/villages for implementing *jhum* control schemes should be confined to a minimum number so that all the schemes may be executed simultaneously in the centres/villages within a duration of 3-4 years in a sustainable manner.

2. Proper motivation to take up the schemes earnestly by the *jhumias* should be endeavoured by the Development Departments.

3. Training courses/demonstration should be organised by the concerned authority to enable the *jhumias* to make better use of the schemes.

4. Monitoring and follow-up action should be undertaken constantly by the scheme implementing agencies. Furthermore, evaluation studies should be conducted by an independent organisation immediately after the completion of the period of the programme.

5. The number of educational institutions should be increased as far as practicable with adequate paraphernalia in order to increase the rate of literacy. Moreover, a course may be included in the academic curriculum to make the students understand about the harmful effects of shifting cultivation.

6. Drinking water facilities should be made available so that the people do not use contaminated water from the rivers, ponds and springs etc.

7. The medi-care institutions available in and around the centres/ villages should be provided with adequate staff, equipments and medicine etc.

8. All weather motorable roads should be constructed for movement of people as well as goods from place to place.

9. Scientific rearing of improved variety of cattle, goats, pigs and poultry etc., for commercial purpose should be made popular among the *jhumias* by the Department of Animal Husbandry and Veterinary.

10. Development of cultured fishery on commercial level by the *jhumias* should be encouraged by the Department of Fisheries with provisions of necessary raw materials and proper technical guidance.

11. Improvement of cottage and small scale industries viz., weaving, bamboo and cane works, sericulture, tailoring and other handicrafts etc.,

is the need of the hour. Provisions for training, grants-in-aid and loans should be made available to the *jhumias*. They should be encouraged to take up these vocations on commercial level.

12. Retail outlets of the Large Area Multipurpose Co-operative Societies (LAMPS) have to be opened up in and around the centres/villages on priority basis and these should be maintained properly.

13. Electricity should be provided to the people not only for domestic consumption but also for agricultural activities.

14. Cadastral survey in the district should be completed as early as possible so that land records of all the villages are readily available.

15. Efforts should be made to popularise the improved technologies as provided by the Agricultural Research Station, Diphu.

16. Development Committees should be constituted by dedicated persons so that the *jhumias* have full faith on them.

17. Proper co-ordination between the Development Departments should be maintained so that the *jhumias* derive desired results out of the schemes. Moreover, there should exist a better relationship between the Development Committee and the Implementing Agencies.

18. At the time of formulation of the plans and programmes for *jhum* control, the views of the social scientists should be taken into consideration.

19. The schemes should be implemented in such a manner that the people do not feel apprehensive of losing their tribal identity in the name of development.

Within the limitations of the present study, in fine, it may be concluded that if the welfare schemes are implemented with sincerity and devotion, the hill tribes of Assam in general and the Karbis in particular are likely to come forward to utilise those for their socio-economic prosperity. This in turn is bound to take the people a step forward towards integrating them with the wider Indian society.

BIBLIOGRAPHY

Agarwal, A.K. 1987. *Economic Problems and Planning in North-east India*. New Delhi : Sterling Publishers Private Ltd.

Bag. G.N. (2001) *Rural Transformation in Tribal Areas,* New Delhi: Akansha Publishing House.

Barkataki, S. 1969. *Tribes of Assam*. New Delhi: National Book Trust, India.

Barman, Kandarpa Kumar. 1990 . 'Shifting Cultivation in the Hills of Assam, in D.N. Majumdar (ed.) *Shifting Cultivation in North-east India*. New Delhi, Omsons Publications, pp. 219 - 228.

Bhattacharjee, Tanmoy. 1986. *Sociology of the Karbis*. Delhi: B.R. Publishing Corporation.

-------- 1990. 'Jhuming in Karbi Anglong', in *Shifting Cultivation in North-east India. D.N. Majumdar (ed.)* New Delhi: Omsons Publications, pp. 229-236.

Bhowmick, P.K. 1990. *Applied-action-development Anthropology*. Calcutta: Institute of Social Research and Applied Anthropology.

Biswas, G.R. 1984. 'Social role for the market', in *(ed.) Marketing in North-east India*. J.B. Ganguly New Delhi: Omsons Publications. pp. 203- 205.

Borah, Durgeswar. 1985 . *Khejurbond* (Socio-economic Resurvey of a Tribal village in North Cachar Hills district of Assam). Jorhat: Agro-

Economic Research Centre for North-east India, Assam Agricultural University.

Borah, Durgeswar. 1992 . 'Constraints of Economic Development in Hilly areas of N.E. India : the Dimasa case', in *Constraints of Economic Development in North-east India*. Edited by P.D. Saikia and Durgeswar Borah. Guwahati : Omsons Publications. pp. 95- 103.

Bordoloi, B.N. 1972 . *District Handbook, United Mikir and North Cachar Hills.* Shillong:Tribal Research Institute.

-------- 1984. The Conceptual aspect of Unemployment in the Context of Tribal Communities of Assam. *Bulletin of the Tribal Research Institute,* Assam, Guwahati, 1: 2 pp.25-33.

Bordoloi, 1985. The Karbis–Their Origin and Migration. *Bulletin of the Tribal Research Institute*, Assam. Guwahati 1 : 3, pp. 55-64.

--------- 1986. 'Problems of transfer and alienation of tribal land in the Karbi Anglong district of Assam with special reference to the Karbis', in *Alienation of tribal land and indebtedness*. Edited by B.N. Bordoloi. Guwahati: Tribal Research Institute, Assam. pp. 120-148.

---------- 1987. 'The Karbis', in *Tribes of Assam Part 1.* Edited by B.N. Bordoloi, G.C. Sharma ,Thakur and M.C. Saikia. Guwahati: Tribal Research Institute, Assam. pp.5-73.

-------- 1990. Tribal development plans and programme in the six scheduled areas of Assam with special reference to management of land–a critical appraisal. *Bulletin of the Assam Institute of Research for Tribals and Scheduled Castes*, Guwahati 1 : 7 pp. 25-42.

--------- 1990. 'The Problems of rehabilitation of the jhumia families in the hill areas of Assam', in *Shifting Cultivation in North-east India.* Edited by D.N. Majumdar. New Delhi: Omsons Publications. pp. 237-242.

---------- 1991. *Transfer and alienation of tribal land in Assam with special reference to the Karbis of the Karbi Anglong district*. Guwahati: B.N. Bordoloi.

Boro, Pradeep. 1996. Environmental Degradation in North-east. *The Sentinel, January 20.* (A Daily published from Guwahati, Assam).

Borthakur, I.K. 1991. 'A strategy to reduce and replace jhum cultivation', in A.K. Dev and S.A. Rizvi *(eds.) Development Programming and Planning in Hill Areas.* Delhi : H.K. Publishers & Distributors, pp.69-93.

Bose, Saradendu, S. Ghatak & R.K. Bera. 1982. 'Shifting cultivation in India', in K.S. Singh *(ed.) Economic of the Tribes and their Transformation*. New Delhi : Concept Publishing Company, pp. 216 - 227.

Chowdhury, J.N. 1992. Land system in hill areas of Assam with special reference to the protection of tribal interest in the land–a seminar paper presented in the seminar held in the Assam Institute of Research for Tribals and Scheduled Castes, Guwahati.

Conklin, Harold C. 1957. *Hanunoo agriculture, report on an integral system of shifting cultivation in the Philippines*. Rome. Food and Agriculture Organization of the United Nations.

Das, B.M. 1987. *The Peoples of Assam,* Delhi: Gyan Publishing House.

Das, B.N. 1997. Socio-economic Backwardness in Assam. *The Assam Tribune, September 29.* (A daily published from Guwahati, Assam).

Das, G.N. 1991. *Report on the survey of socio-economic conditions of the scheduled tribe population living within Mini Compact Areas in the autonomous hill districts of Assam (Miyungdisa MCAP).* (Unpublished). Diphu: District Research Office.

-------- 1991. *Report on the survey of socio-economic conditions of the scheduled tribe population living within Mini Compact Areas in the autonomous hill districts of Assam (Hidipi MCAP).* (Unpublished). Diphu:District Research Office.

---------- 1992. *Report on the survey of socio-economic conditions of the scheduled tribe population living within Compact Areas in the autonomous hill districts of Assam (Samelangso-Rongmongve CADP).* (Unpublished). Diphu: District Research Office.

Das, G.N. 1997. 'Impact of the central sector jhum control programme in the hill areas of Assam', *in People of the Himalayas ecology, culture, development and change.* Edited by K.C. Mahanta. Delhi: Kamala-Raj Enterprises, pp.237-241.

Das, M.M. 1984. *Peasant Agriculture in Assam.* New Delhi:Inter-India Publications.

Das, N.K. 1987. *Ethnic Identity Ethnicity and Social Stratification in North-east India.* New Delhi: Inter-India Publications.

Devi, L. 1992 . *Ahom-Tribal Relations (a political study).* Guwahati: Lawyer's Book Stall.

District Council, Karbi Anglong. 1987. *The Karbi Anglong autonomous district council* code. Diphu.

---------- 1988. *Project Report on Integrated Jhumia Development Programme.* Diphu.

District Council, N.C. Hills. 1988. *Project Report on Integrated Jhumia Development Programme.* Haflong.

------------ 1989. *Brief Note of Evaluation of Boromoulkoi.* Haflong.

Dutt, K.N. 1979. *Gazetteer of India Assam State, U.M. & N.C. Hills district (Karbi Anglong & North Cachar hills districts).* Gauhati: The Editor-in-Chief, District Gazetteers, Government of Assam.

Dutta, Parul. 1989. *Arunachal Pradesh, An Overview.* Itanagar: Government of Arunachal Pradesh.

Elwin, Verrier, 1964. *A Philosophy for NEFA*. Shillong: Govt. of Assam.

Gohain, B.C. 1994 . '*Shifting cultivation among the Abors', in Tribal life in India*. Edited by Devendra Kumar and D.N. Thakur. New Delhi: Deep & Deep Publications. pp. 180-191.

Gohain, B. K. 1984. *The Hill Karbis*. Diphu: Arunima Gohain.

Gohain, Debasish. 1969. 'The socio-economic survey of Mawtnum (1963-64)', in *Rural life in Assam hills, case studies of four villages*. Jorhat:Agro-Economic Research Centre for N.E. India.

Goswami, Promod. 1994. Shifting cultivation of the hill tribes of Assam. *Bulletin of Assam Institute of Research for Tribals and Scheduled Castes*, Guwahati. 1 : 9 pp. 8-10.

Goswami, P.C. & N. Saha. 1969. *A study on the problems of agricultural development in the hill areas of N.E. India*. Jorhat: Agro-Economic Research Centre for N.E. India.

Government of Assam. 1988. *Hasao bubli–news bulletin*. Haflong : Directorate of Information & Public Relations, Assam (H).

---------- 1991. *A status paper on the central sector jhum control programme in hill areas of Assam*. Dispur:Development Commissioner for Hill Areas.

---------- *Draft eighth five year plan 1992-97, Vol.7*, Raman Dispur: Development Commissioner for Hill Areas, pp. JA1-2.

------------ 1997. *Report on the status of primary education in Karbi Anglong district*. Guwahati:Assam Institute of Research for Tribals and Scheduled Castes.

Hazarika, M.P. 1988. Shifting Cultivation-A perennial problem in the North-east. *Journal of the North-eastern Council*, Shillong. 9:3 pp.17-19.

Jha, S.D. 1988. *Socio-economic and Demographic Dimension of Arunachal Pradesh.* New Delhi: Omsons Publications.

Kar, R.K. 1986. Shifting cultivation: an appraisal with special reference to North-east India. *Bul letin of the Department of Anthropology,* Dibrugarh University, Dibrugarh. 15 : pp. 38 - 62.

----------- 1994 . 'The Tribes of North-east India: An overview in Sarthak Sengupta *(ed.) Tribes of North-east India.*New Delhi: Gian Publishing House, pp. 1- 20.

Kathar, J.I. 1988. A brief note on Karbi language. *The Emissary, April 15.* (A Fortnightly published from Diphu).

Lyall, Charles. 1971. *The Mikirs.* Guwahati: United Publishers.

Majumdar, D.N. 1982. 'An appraisal of the tribal situation in North east India', in Pankaj Thakur (ed.) *India's North-east.* Tinsukia: Prakash Publishing House, pp. 126-142

---------- 1990. 'An assessment of shifting cultivation in North-east India', in D.N. Majumdar (ed.) *Shifting cultivation in North-east India.* New Delhi : Omsons Publications, pp. 22- 32.

Medhi, B.K. 1988. The Karbi society at a glance. *Souvenir of the Anthropological Society of North-east India, XXIII Annual Session.* Edited by H.C. Sharma and T.K. Sharma. Guwahati: General Secretary, ASNEI. pp. 8-13.

Nath, Rajmohan. 1978 . *The Background of Assames Culture.* Guwahati: Lawyer's Book Stall.

Pegu, S.S. 1980. 'Diphu: A study in urban growth', in S.M. Dubey, P.K. Bordoloi & B.N. Borthakur (ed.) *Family, Marriage and social change on the Indian Fringe.* New Delhi : Cosmo Publications, pp. 196 - 206.

Phangsho, P. 1984. 'Traces of Austric and Aryan influences on the Karbis', *Journal of North-east India Council for Social Science Research.* Shillong. 8:2 pp. 32-35.

Prasad, R.N., A. Singh & Arun Varma. 1990. 'Shifting cultivation and land degradation', in *D.N. Majumdar* (ed). *Shifting cultivation in North-east India.* New Delhi: Omsons Publications. pp, 143-158.

Ray, D. 1969. 'Socio-Economic Survey of Kanther Terang', in *Rural life in Assam hills, case studies of four villages.* Jorhat: Agro-Economic Research Centre for N.E. India.

Roy Burman, B.K. 1970 . *Census of India, 1961, demographic and socio-economic profiles of the hill areas of North-east India.* New Delhi: Office of the Registrar General, India, Ministry of Home Affairs.

----------1982. *Report of Committee on Forest and Tribals in India. September.* New Delhi: Ministry of Home Affairs, Govt. of India.

---------- 1989. Critical appraisal of Shiftihng Cultivation Farming Technology and of various Approaches. *Journal of the North-Eastern Council,* Shillong. 10 : 2-3. pp.1- 4.

Sachan, A.K. 1990. 'Constraints of Tribal Development', in *B.N. Bordoloi, (ed.) Constraints of Tribal Development in North-east India.* Guwahati : Tribal Research Institute, Assam. pp.160-167.

Sachchidananda, 1988. 'Tradition and development in Arunachal Pradesh', in Sachchidananda, B.B. Mandal, K.K. Verma and R.P. Sinha (ed.) *Tradition and Development.* New Delhi: Concept Publishing Company. pp. 53-62.

----------- 1989 . *Shifting Cultivation in India.* New Delhi : Concept Publishing Company.

Saha, N. & M.D. Barkataky. 1969 . Socio-economic Survey of Banshidua', in *Rural Life in Assam Hills, Case studies of four villages.* Jorhat: Agro-Economic Research Centre for N.E. India.

Saikia, M.C. 1984. *Report on the working of the gaon panchayat level co-operative societies in the tribal subplan areas and LAMPS in the hill areas of Assam*. Guwahati: Tribal Research Institute, Assam.

Saikia, P.D. 1968. *Changes in Mikir Society, A case study of Kanther Terang village, Mikir hills, Assam*. Jorhat: Agro-Economic Research Centre for N.E. India.

Saikia, P.D. & Durgeswar Borah. 1992. *Constraints of Economic Development in North-east India*. Guwahati : Omsons Publications.

Sarma, N.N., S.R. Paul and D. Sarma. 1996. Positive approaches to the Shifting Cultivation in the Hills Zone of Assam, a paper presented in the seminar on *Tribal Tradition and its Relation to Development in the Hill Areas of Assam,* held in the Assam Institute of Research for Tribals and Scheduled Castes, Guwahati on 19 - 21 Sept '96.

Sharma, A.K. 1989. *Issues in Social Demography*. Delhi: Mittal Publications.

Sharma, U.C. & R.N. Prasad. 1994. Socio-economic considerations in enhancing agricultural productivity in North -eastern states, *IASSI Quarterly* (New Delhi) 12 : 34, pp. 6-16.

Sharma Thakur, G.C. 1990. Rehabilitation of the Jhumiyas, A case study of a tribal village in Karbi Anglong', in D.N. Majumdar (ed.) *Shifting Cultivation in North-east India.* New Delhi: Omsons Publications, pp. 243-246.

Srivastava, S.C. 1987. *Demographic Profile of North-east India*. Delhi : Mittal Publications.

Terang, Rong Bong. 1982 . Karbi lullaby : A petal of folklore. *The Assam Tribune, April 23* . (A Daily published from Guwahati, Assam).

Teron, Lankam, 1974. *Karbi Janagosthi.* Jorhat : Assam Sahitya Sabha.

----------- 1996. A few social custom of the Karbi. *The Assam Tribune, April 30.* (A Daily published from Guwahati, Assam).

Vidyarthi, L.P. 1986. *Art and Culture of North-east India*. New Delhi: Publications Division, Ministry of Information and Broadcasting, Government of India.

Other sources

The Assam Tribune (A Daily published from Guwahati, Assam) News items in issues dated 6 May, 1996 and 10 March, 1997.

INDEX